"NO BROILED FOOD"

—— *on the menu of the*
Edisto Motel Restaurant,
Jacksonboro, South Carolina

THE FEARLESS FRYING COOKBOOK

THE
FEARLESS
FRYING
COOKBOOK

BY HOPPIN' JOHN MARTIN TAYLOR

ILLUSTRATIONS BY PETER ALSBERG

WORKMAN PUBLISHING, NEW YORK

Library of Congress Cataloging-in-Publication Data
Taylor, John Martin
Fearless Frying Cookbook / by Hoppin' John Martin Taylor;
illustrations by Peter Alsberg.
        p. cm.
Includes index.
ISBN 1-56305-847-2 (pbk.)
1. Frying. 2. Cookery, International.
TX689.T39 1997
641 . 7 '7–dc21   97-20189
                                                    CIP

Cover design by Paul Gamarello
Book design by Paul Gamarello with Barbara Balch
Author photograph by Anthony Lowe
Food photographs by Louis Wallach

Workman books are available at special discounts when purchased
in bulk for premiums and sales promotions as well as for fund-
raising or educational use. Special editions or book excerpts can
be created to specification. For details, contact the Special Sales
Director at the address below.

Workman Publishing Company, Inc.
708 Broadway
New York, NY 10003-9555

Manufactured in the United States of America
First printing July 1997
10 9 8 7 6 5 4 3

FOR ZELMA

AND

LANIER HICKMAN

AND

DORIS COOK

ACKNOWLEDGMENTS

I am indebted to many people who lent their support and wisdom during the writing of this book. Foremost, to Mikel Herrington and my sister Sue Highfield and to my dear friend Debbie Marlowe.

Thanks also to Carolan Workman who waited for me to finish other projects before beginning this one, to my agent Doe Coover, and to my editor at Workman, Suzanne Rafer. Also at Workman, I'd like to thank the following: Kathie Ness, Carrie Schoen, and Emily Nolan, in the editorial department; designers Paul Gamarello and Barbara Balch; publicist Deborah DeLosa; and marketing manager Andrea Glickson.

Thanks to Fran McCullough for her continued support and understanding as well as some great recipes.

This book is the result of the kindness and generosity of many great fry cooks. Many of these recipes are my versions of recipes that have appeared elsewhere in print. I am indebted to the writers— some of them accomplished chefs as well— Madeline Kamman, Nancie McDermott, Mardee Regan, Zarela Martinez, Jasper White, Nicole Routhier, Jessica Harris, Karen Hess, Steve Raichlen, Jeff Steingarten, Mark Miller (and his assistant Leland Atkinson), Stephan Pyles (and his assistant Kellye Milner), Carol Field, Bruce Aidells, John Egerton, Nick Malgieri, George Germon and Johanne Killeen, Marion Cunningham, Rose Levy Beranbaum, Lucy Seligman, Paula Wolfert, Elisabeth Luard, Barbara Kafka, Virginia Elverson, Shirley Corriher, Bharti Kirchner, Jeanne Voltz, and the late Richard Sax.

Chefs Jimmy Sneed, Frank Stitt, Kim-Anh Huebner, Philip Bardin, JoAnn Yaeger, Chris Hastings, Jamie Shannon, Scott Fales, Michael McNally, and Rob Enniss are all masters of the frying pan and have been helpful, as have restaurateurs JoAnn Clevenger and Celia Cerasoli. Celia's mother, Tina ("Mommy"), showed me how to make her inimitable *sfingi* in my minuscule kitchen, then she and Arnold ("Daddy") proofread a recipe that they had never before seen written. Celia's chef Donna Gustafson checked the recipe to make sure I had it right. And Donna Florio and Robert Barbato, two more fine Italian cooks from Charleston, continue to offer their recipes and friendship. In Apulia, everyone in the small walled village of Acaya opened their doors to this stranger, as did Tina and Marcello Lagrua at Trattoria Casareccia in Lecce.

Jan Newberry of Taunton's *Fine Cooking* magazine early on recognized the importance of this project and hired me to write about frying; some information has appeared there in a somewhat different version.

None of this would have happened if it weren't for the perfect fried fish at the Edisto Motel Restaurant in Jacksonboro, South Carolina. Thanks to Zelma, Lanier, and Michael Hickman, Doris Cook, and all the gang there.

George and Cecilia Holland continue to provide me with the wonderful corn products that make frying so much tastier, and my friends at Crosby's Seafood never scrimp on quality or service. Any time I need fresh lard, I can rely on Frank Marvin in Hollywood, South Carolina. Jack and Andrea Limehouse managed to find the most beautiful produce even when California was flooded. Having these kind and reliable suppliers has made testing recipes a much more enjoyable process.

And last but not least, special thanks to Roy Finamore, Bessie Hanahan, Lucille Grant, Scot Hinson, Marion Sams, Bruce Love and the B-52's.

CONTENTS

INTRODUCTION

GOOD FRIED FOOD

This book began several years ago in the Edisto Motel Restaurant in tiny Jacksonboro, South Carolina. It was in fact late winter, but here on the Carolina coast that means sweater weather, and I remember riding down Highway 17 with the car windows open a little to let in the early spring balm. Jacksonboro nestles up to a bend in the black and sinuous Edisto River and stops the divided highway nearly dead in its tracks. From here south the famed Ocean Highway, once the major north-south route from New York to Miami, must meander on a two-lane blacktop through the real lowcountry—saltmarsh and live oaks, old rice fields and palmettos—until it reaches the developers' "plantations" and the divided highway reemerges only to deliver you onto the bold concrete of I-95.

I was with Carolan Workman of Workman Publishing, and we had come to eat at the Edisto, a plain cinder-block building a half-hour south of Charleston, where Zelma Hickman and her family have been serving fried food for fifty years. It's one of my favorite places to take out-of-towners—typically lowcountry, open on Thursdays, Fridays, and Saturdays only, where the menu boasts, "No Broiled Food," and where people have been known to stand in line for hours to taste the perfectly fried flounder, catfish, shad, roe, shrimp, and oysters.

I was explaining my battlecry for deep fried foods to Carolan—that as long as you use clean, hot oil and don't crowd the fryer, deep frying is a dry cooking technique that produces elegant, greaseless foods with crisp coatings and succulent interiors. A plate of shrimp arrived: not one drop of grease on the food or on the plate. "You southerners really do know how to fry," Carolan exclaimed as she examined the lightly breaded shrimp on her platter. "Why don't you write a book about it!"

I took a bite of the hushpuppy and considered her offer. Although I had two books to finish before I could possibly start frying, I excitedly agreed to write this book. I don't think either of us imagined anything at all like the book that you now hold. I quickly realized that "deep" and "southern" aren't the only fried foods in this world, and that the book would evolve a world of frying not southern at all.

Quite simply, the great truth is that everyone loves good fried food—and not just poultry and fish. Fritters, wontons, croquettes, chips, beignets, noodles, doughnuts, and potatoes come to mind. Chiles rellenos and tempura and spring rolls. Okra and green tomatoes. As I started to work on this book, I recalled lacy fried elderflower blossoms from Austria, great *pommes frites* in Paris, spicy meat-and coconut-filled patties in the Caribbean, and whole fish in my favorite Asian restaurant.

To help me along, I wrote to my colleagues—fellow cookbook authors and restaurateurs whose work I respect and whose recipes I wanted to include in this collection. The outpouring of support was infectious—none more enthusiastic than Nancie McDermott's 20-page letter, brimming with recipes. Nancie is a fellow southerner who now resides in California where she teaches the Asian cooking she learned when she was in the Peace Corps in Thailand. Her cookbook, *Real Thai,* is one of my favorites. "If this is overkill," she told me in her first of several letters about frying, "then there it is. I am, after all, a good Southern girl who traipsed off to Asia, that other bastion of hot grease and guilt-free feasting."

As my colleagues responded, what emerged was not only a worldwide devotion to fried foods, but also a new world order of frying—an international, cross-cultural style that blended the ingredients and techniques of different nations: tempura batters enlivened with cornmeal; chips made from all sorts of root vegetables, not just potatoes; Indian chickpea fritters made with continental greens; chili peppers in pasta dough; and fried fish encrusted with nuts and herbs.

I know that Madison Avenue and the news media have convinced many Americans that fried foods are bad for you, but I just don't buy into it. I would bet, moreover, that it's a lack of common sense that produces bad health, not the foods we eat. It stands to reason that you can't eat a typical nineteenth century farmer's breakfast of fried eggs, fried pancakes, fried bacon, and syrup, then go sit behind a desk all day and expect anything other than a broadened backside and hardened arteries. But don't blame the fried foods and don't blame the fats! For years we were told that processed vegetable shortening was better for us than animal fats; now the experts say that the hydrogenation process creates trans-fats that create more cholesterol than the saturated fats in poultry.

It's always been my contention that you can pretty much eat what you want as long as you do so in moderation and in conjunction with exercise. Americans eat far too many processed foods with hidden ingredients and questionable processing techniques such as the aforementioned hydrogenation. Further, organically grown produce contains as much as 75% more nutrients than those picture-perfect products of agri-business, yet few of us bother to seek it out, even as we carefully watch our diets.

Nearly every "lay" person I've mentioned this book to has looked at me incredulously and asked, "How do you stay so thin?" They are not trying to say that I am skinny (I'm not), but that they believe that fried foods are fatty and that they will automatically make you fat. I find this truly amusing in light of the fact that the professionals—the cooks, cookbook writers, and waiters—I've discussed it with say, almost without exception, that the fried dishes are the most popular ones in their restaurants. As Nancie said, "We love fried foods, y'all, and it's all around the world since the evolution of the pot and the pan."

She wasn't kidding. From the Azores to Alaska, recipes for fried foods appear in every culture. In truth, techniques vary little and everywhere there seems to be the local version of an international favorite such as fried dough.

Nevertheless, as I combed my favorite cookbooks in search of great recipes for fried foods, I almost never found the word "fried" in the indexes, even when the books included delicious fritters, doughnuts, chips, and croquettes. Nancie McDermott encouraged me to "Give them low-life low-fat tomes a run for their money and tell the truth." And so it's as much to set the record straight as to offer these delicious recipes that I wrote this book. In every kitchen I looked in I found wonderful fried food—but nary a fat cook. Jeanne Voltz, the barbecue expert and redoubtable southern food writer, told me from her home in North Carolina, "Even I cut back on fat sometimes, but I do it in the privacy of my own home and don't tell anyone about it."

I don't pretend that all frying is fat-free. Indeed, sautéing aims to add fat to the dish being fried. As Karen Hess, the culinary historian, has so wryly, wisely noted, "Cholesterol is flavor!" Of course, we could all ignore the amounts of cholesterol in our diet if we would exercise more; better yet if we could choose our grandparents according to their serum cholesterol counts. But life is too short to do without flavor, so I offer this book smack dab in the face of conventional wisdom with the hopes that you will try these recipes without guilt. It's probably the most fun cooking you can do—and it's certainly the fastest.

—John Martin Taylor
Charleston, 1997

FEARLESS FRYING RECIPES

CHAPTER 1

GETTING STARTED

References to frying appear in ancient manuscripts in both the East and the West, although no one can pinpoint the origin of the technique of cooking in hot oil. The evolution of frying as a cooking method probably closely follows the development of metal pots. Today we take so many of our modern conveniences for granted that we forget that the modern western kitchen, unimaginable a hundred years ago, is still unheard of in much of the world. Accurate thermometers, rheostats, and thermostats are recent luxuries. Sautéing, for example, appeared only after stoves with variable heat sources appeared in the nineteenth century. Frying, then, as we know it, is very modern cooking.

In this chapter we'll look at the basic techniques of deep-frying, pan-frying and sautéing, and stir-frying. Recommendations for equipment, some facts about fats and oils, and a few helpful hints are included to help relieve any "fears of frying" you might have. Basic batters and breadings are described, but each recipe in the book is self-contained. Read this chapter through, then thumb through the book to find recipes for the most delicious fried morsels imaginable.

DEEP-FRYING,
THE PERFECT MEDIUM

There's hardly a person among us who can resist perfectly fried onion rings, French fries, hushpuppies, or doughnuts. When cooked to perfection in clean, hot oil, deep-fried foods are crisp on the outside and moist and tender on the inside. They should not be greasy at all—not even a drop of oil on the plates that hold them.

When it is deep-fried, the food is surrounded by very hot fat (over 100 degrees hotter than boiling water), which sears the exterior by caramelizing the natural sugars in the food. The sizzling noise is the instantaneous vaporization of water as it hits the hot oil. Baking, broiling, and grilling can be done at hotter temperatures, but only in deep-frying is the heat so directly transferred to the food. The cooking is fast and, as long as the food is properly prepared, even.

Deep-frying is the perfect way to cook foods that don't have a dense or fibrous structure, such as many seafoods, vegetables, and batters. It is also an ideal medium for cooking croquettes and fritters made of foods that have previously been cooked. There are no great secrets to deep-frying—just a handful of rules.

1. Read the recipe all the way through and assemble all the tools and ingredients before you begin.

2. Always use clean oil. You can use the vegetable oil of your choice, but I generally recommend peanut oil for deep-frying. It has a high smoking point and lasts longer (is more stable) than most. Most animal fats will burn, or reach the smoking point, when heated to 375°F; some vegetable oils have a smoking point as high as 450°F. Those that have been hydrogenated and those that contain preservatives and emulsifiers, such as commercial vegetable shortenings, have much lower smoking points. The smoking point is lowered every time a fat is used.

3. Choose a pot that is larger than the heat source. Oil catches fire easily, so you want to avoid any spilling. Cast iron conducts heat evenly and holds it well, but most cast-iron skillets aren't deep enough for true deep-frying. A cast-iron Dutch oven, however, makes a good frying pot. The larger the surface area, the faster the decomposition of the oil, so manufacturers have designed electric deep-fryers that are tall and narrow. One disadvantage to this type is that they don't hold much food at one time. Also, many electric fryers do not have a thermostat; shop accordingly.

4. Never fill a pot more than half full of oil. You'll need at least 3 inches between the surface of the oil and the top of the pot to allow room for the oil to bubble up.

5. Constantly monitor the temperature. You'll need a high-quality candy or deep-frying thermometer (available in restaurant supply houses if your local grocer or kitchenware shop doesn't stock one) that accurately measures temperatures from 325° to 450°F. Buy one that is designed with a metal sheath that prevents anything but liquids from touching the graduated glass tube; you'll want one with a clamp on it as well, so that you can attach it to the side of the pot. Place the thermometer in the oil and turn the heat to the required temperature. Do not put the heat source to its highest setting; you'll want more leeway when the frying begins. The instant the oil reaches that temperature, add the food. Carefully maintain the temperature throughout the frying. Most deep-frying is done around 365°F (just remember the number of days

in a year). If you find yourself without a thermometer, drop a cube of home-style white bread into the hot oil: at 350°F the bread fries to a golden brown in about 1 minute; at 375°F, it takes about 40 seconds. A few raw doughs can be fried crisp at temperatures slightly lower than 340°F, but they are the exception. Follow the temperatures indicated in each recipe.

6. Do not crowd the pot. Add only as much food as the pot can hold without the pieces touching. The oil should bubble up freely around each piece, and the temperature should not drop.

7. Use proper tools for adding and removing foods. Some fryers come with frying baskets that allow you to lower and raise the foods all at once. Baskets have two disadvantages: adding all of the food to the oil at the same time can cause the temperature to suddenly drop below 340°F, at which point the food will absorb the oil and become greasy; also, batters often stick to the baskets. I use long spring-loaded tongs, an Oriental wire mesh skimmer, or a slotted utensil made expressly for the purpose (mine, a Kitcha-majig, was my mother's; it's still being manufactured). Avoid slotted spoons; oil often gathers in them.

If you dip your utensil in the hot oil before picking up foods to be fried, batters and breadings won't stick.

8. Remove the foods in the exact order in which they were added to the pot so that they are all evenly cooked.

9. Drain the fried foods well of all grease. The advantage of fryer baskets is that they usually have a hook that suspends the pot over the oil, where any excess grease can drain off. If you're not using a basket, simply hold each piece of food over the pot for a moment, turning it

so that all grease drips back into the pot; then place the fried food on a wire rack that is placed over a baking sheet, where it will drain further. Do *not* place the food on paper towels or on brown paper unless the recipe tells you to do so.

10. Keep the food warm while you prepare the next batch. Few fried foods can be prepared in one batch. Have an

TWO EXCEPTIONS TO THE RULE

While most foods must be fried at a high temperature, I have found two exceptions to the rule in my search for the world's best fried foods: raw nuts and small oily fish. Both the nuts and the fish are so oily themselves that they don't absorb additional oil. Harold McGee, an expert on kitchen science, says that nuts can be fried as low as 275°F. And Paula Wolfert, one of the world's best food writers and an authority on Mediterranean cuisines, found eastern Mediterranean cooks frying small sardines and baby red mullets at 300°F: "These two- and three-inch-long fish weigh about ¾ ounce, cook at the bottom of the pan, then rise when done, emerging crisp, golden, juicy, and oil-free. The olive oil used to fry them may be used many times, since it is never allowed to reach its smoke point." Paula also offers this tip: "To store olive oil for reuse, cool and strain it through cheese-cloth that has been wrung out in vine-gared water. Store in a cool place."

oven preheated to its lowest setting and simply place the food—sitting on a wire rack that is set on a baking sheet—in the oven while you continue frying.

11. Always follow all *of these rules with each batch.* And before you begin the next batch, remove any particles of food from the oil to prevent them from burning the next time around. Make sure the oil has come back up to the proper temperature before frying subsequent batches.

12. If, at any time, the oil begins to smoke, discard it and start again. It is burned and will impart a smoky taste.

13. Always allow the oil to cool before attempting to move it. When the oil is no longer hot enough to burn you, filter it into a clean pot. I use a large coffee filter set in a large sieve. When the filtered oil has cooled completely, pour it into a container with a tight-fitting lid and store it in a cool, dark place. If you have fried strongly scented and flavored foods, you can try to "clarify" the oil by putting several slices of raw potato in the cooled oil and reheating it slowly, stirring occasionally, until the oil reaches about 350°F or the potato starts to brown. Discard the potato and strain again. Before reusing oil, simply smell it to see if it is still fresh-smelling. If it's not, discard it. You'll find that unsaturated fats go bad more quickly than saturated fats.

14. Always cool the oil to room temperature before disposing it. When the oil can no longer be reused, cool it and carefully pour it into an empty ½-gallon juice or milk carton. Then it is ready to be discarded.

ABOUT BREADINGS AND BATTERS

Now that you know *how* to deep-fry, you can proceed to fry all sorts of foods, from individual herb leaves to entire turkeys. Delicate foods must be coated with breadings or batters; uncoated foods, such as potatoes, must be perfectly dry. Some foods, such as fish fillets and poultry, fry perfectly with a light dusting of flour or corn flour; others need denser coatings to protect them while they fry. A common breading throughout the world is a dusting of flour followed by a dip in an egg wash and then bread crumbs. Cubes of cheese, vegetables, and fragile seafoods are often breaded in this manner.

Batters are also internationally popular coatings. Thick enough to coat the foods they protect but thin enough to pour, they are usually made with eggs beaten into flour or another starch. Ice-cold water is added to Japanese tempura, the lightest batter of all; milk adds a silken quality and browns more easily. A rich *palacsinta* (a Hungarian pancake) batter made with cream is perfect for desserts such as fried bananas. If coated with dry bread crumbs, the coating will be crisp as well. Oil is added to some batters to keep fritters from sticking to pans and utensils. Yeast and baking powder are included in others to lighten the batters of quickly cooked foods. Salt, pepper, and cayenne often season the breadings or batters, but avoid adding delicate dried herbs or sugar, both of which will burn before the food is cooked. All of the recipes in this book include complete instructions for the batter within the recipe.

SAUTEING AND PAN-FRYING

*S*auter means, among other things, "to jump" in French. Its use as a culinary term didn't come about until stovetops with adjustable settings were invented. In classic French cooking, the term was originally applied only to foods that were cut into equal sizes and cooked in hot fat without first being floured; liquids are sometimes added to the pan to either finish the cooking or to deglaze the pan for a sauce.

Sautéing is a form of frying. Some etymologists say that the foods are cooked at a high temperature so that they jump in the pan; others insist that the term evolved because the pan is sometimes shaken so that the foods jump. Either way, you'll need a hot pan in which the foods can be tossed, stirred, or turned easily. Many cooks prefer pans with sloping sides, but the classic French *sauteuse* is a heavy flat-bottomed pan with a strong handle, straight sides, and a lid. One of the best pieces of equipment you can buy for your kitchen, a French stainless-steel-lined copper sauté pan is an extravagance worth owning.

The biggest difference between sautéing and frying is that you *want* sautéed foods to be moistened and flavored by the fat. As the great 19th-century French

A NOTE ABOUT COMMERCIAL FRYERS

Hardly a restaurant today is without a deep-fryer. It is often a very expensive thermostatically-controlled machine that keeps a huge quantity of oil at just the right temperature; some have elaborate filtration systems to keep the oil fresh and clean. If you see a drop of oil on your plate under the food you order, send it back. There is no excuse for this in a restaurant.

There are also wonderfully designed deep-fryers on the market for the home cook, but I find that they don't hold very much food. They all have thermostats, and some have filters that prevent greasy fumes from escaping into the air, but if you have a good ventilation system (or fry outdoors, the way I often do) and an accurate thermometer, there is no need to purchase an electric fryer. All of the deep-frying recipes in this book work perfectly well with electric deep-fryers; just be sure to follow all of the rules.

Electric skillets have adjustable thermostats and are good for pan-frying some foods, but they don't hold enough oil for deep-frying. Electric woks, on the other hand, while not powerful enough to maintain the high temperatures necessary for the stir-frying for which they were designed, are good for deep-frying because they have adjustable thermostats as well as a surface area that is wider than the base, allowing deep-frying to be accomplished in less oil than is required for pots with the same base and surface areas. They can also be placed away from the stove, where other cooking is likely to be going on.

chef Alexis Soyer noted, "The word frying is often wrongly used in cookery instead of the word sauté. . . . Sauté means anything cooked in a very small amount of butter, oil, lard, or fat, on one side of the article at a time, whereas the other requires about a hundred times more of the aforementioned materials to cook properly."

Butter is the traditional fat that gives the nutty flavor and golden color to the classic French preparation *à la meunière* ("in the style of the miller's wife"), which usually refers to fish dusted with flour before browning. Clarified butter (see box) is used when you do not want the butter to burn. Duck fat, lard, and olive oil are also commonly used; it is said that you can divide France into regions according to the fat used in sautéing. The fats provide flavor to bland foods such as potatoes, but there should not be so much as to overpower the food being sautéed; there should be just enough fat to coat the bottom of the pan and keep the food from sticking.

The fat should also be hot enough to brown the food and seal in the juices. In order to brown, the outside of the food should be perfectly dry; dusting with flour ensures a dry coating that facilitates the browning. To test the temperature of fat, add a small piece of the food to the pan: the fat should bubble freely all around it.

Pan-frying is really only a catchall term for most frying that isn't done in deep fat. Pan-frying can mean sautéing or it can mean shallow-frying, in which the foods are cooked in a little more fat (though never more than

CLARIFIED BUTTER

Clarified butter is pure golden butterfat, with none of the milk solids that cause butter to brown and burn. It is utter simplicity to make: Melt butter in a saucepan over low heat until it is completely liquid. It will separate into three layers: a foamy surface, the golden butterfat, and a milky residue on the bottom. Skim the foam from the surface and discard it; then slowly pour the butterfat into another container, leaving the milky layer behind.

If you have another buttery dish or sauce that is not being sautéed, you can add the cull (the milky residue) to that dish; otherwise, discard it.

One stick (4 ounces) of butter loses about 1 tablespoon of volume in clarifying; the resulting amount is enough to cover the bottom of an 8- to 10-inch sauté pan by about ¼ inch. Clarified butter keeps, covered and refrigerated, for several weeks.

one third the depth of the pan) and a little more quickly in order to sear the outside. Shallow-frying is essentially the same as deep-frying: a "dry" technique of browning the outside of the food while heating (or reheating) the inside. Shallow-fried foods should be drained of excess grease and may need to be placed on, or patted dry with, paper towels.

Another form of pan-frying is the dry-frying of fatty foods with no additional fat. There are two methods of dry-frying. In one, fatty foods such as bacon or sausages are arranged in a cold skillet and then placed over the heat; the fat is poured off as it is released from the food. In the other, the pan is preheated as if it were a grill, and the foods, such as steaks or duck breasts, are added to the hot pan to sear the outside; the temperature is then usually turned down a little to finish the cooking. Many cookbook authors recommend heavy nonstick pans for dry-frying, but I use the same old, well-seasoned cast-iron skillet that I use for much of my cooking. It is an invaluable kitchen tool. If you don't have one, go buy one and follow the directions on page 10 for seasoning it.

STIR-FRYING

Stir-frying in a wok is Asia's brilliant solution to its age-old problems of scarcities of both fuel and food. Cooking small pieces of food in a small amount of very hot fat that coats the concave surface of the energy-efficient pot is no less than engineering genius. Foods chopped into uniform pieces cook quickly as they are tossed around in the wok, constantly in contact with the hot surface. Often a liquid, lightly thickened with cornstarch, is added to the pan near the end of the cooking time to bind the one-pot meal together, forming a sauce.

Stir-frying recipes usually spell out each step in detail; there's no special technique to master. What's important is to have all the ingredients measured and prepared in advance. A more elaborate Asian meal can begin with a simple clear soup, followed by spring rolls fried in the wok, and then the quickly stir-fried main course served over rice—a matter of timing and advance preparation, but nothing difficult.

ON CAST IRON AND LARD

No pan knows as many uses as a well-seasoned cast-iron skillet. I have one that was my mother's and another that was my grandmother's. I have several others, too, that I have acquired over the years for specific tasks. I prefer to use large cast-iron pots when I fry—the bigger, the better. Cast iron conducts heat evenly and holds it for a long time. The larger the quantity of oil, the easier it is to maintain its temperature.

For deep-frying, the pot should be wider than the heat source and deep enough to hold 2 inches of oil which can bubble freely without overflowing. Dutch ovens are fine, but I have one big rectangular cast-iron pot that is 4 inches deep, 12 inches wide, and 20 inches long. It fits perfectly over two burners of a standard stove. A gallon of oil fills it 1½ inches deep.

Sometimes you can find used well-seasoned cast-iron pots in antique and junk stores. Skillets with a good patina should have a clean, shiny black interior. If you buy new cast iron, wash it once with soap and water, then render some lard in it. Rendering lard is a perfect way to "season" your cast iron, and it's incredibly simple: Have your butcher save clean fresh pork fat for you. The butcher may also be willing to run it through a meat grinder to save you a step. Put a mere film of water in the bottom of the pan. Grind or dice the fat, and add it to the pan. Put the pan over very low heat or in an oven preheated to 225°F. Melt the fat slowly. It can take an hour or more. When the solid matter, or cracklings, turns brown and sinks to the bottom of the pan, strain the lard through several layers of cheesecloth, or through a fine-mesh stainless-steel strainer, into sterilized jars or a large, rather flat plastic container with a tight-fitting lid. Cover the containers with cheesecloth to keep out dust, but do not cap them for two days. Covered, the lard will last for several months in a cool, dark place and even longer in the refrigerator.

After you have rendered the lard, wipe out the pan—but be sure to never wash it again with soap. After each use, paint the inside of the cast-iron pan with lard or bacon grease, and then wipe it out. If you must wash it, use cold water and a natural bristle brush. Always wipe the greased pan; admire the shiny black patina and know that you're halfway to being a real fry cook.

CHAPTER 2

BREADS AND BATTERS

Who among us doesn't love bread and griddlecakes? French toast and breakfast pancakes were two of the first dishes I learned to make as a child, and I'm still fond of them when a hearty breakfast is the only proper start for a cool morning. Variations on these timeless, simple recipes made with grains are found throughout the world. In this chapter there are pancakes, blini, sopaipillas, tortilla chips, and croutons, all attesting to the international love of fried breads and batters.

Here fresh corn is added to a delicate batter and shaped into little patties that I love to serve alongside stewed meats; dried and ground, corn appears in the simple tortilla chips that we take for granted at parties, or in delicious refried grits, ready to be topped with your favorite sauce (another similar but more informal preparation are hushpuppies that appear in the Fish and Shellfish chapter). Many of these recipes are old favorites from my childhood, but others, such as blini and chickpea fritters, are foods that I've grown fond of as I've expanded my culinary horizons. The next time you want to brighten a meal with exciting new tastes and textures, fry up some of these!

FRENCH TOAST

SERVES 4

In New Orleans, they call French toast *pain perdu* (lost bread), for the day-old baguette that otherwise would be thrown out. (I never throw out leftover baguettes because they dry rock-hard and can be grated to make coarse bread crumbs that are a perfect coating for fried foods.) French toast is best when made the New Orleans way, with day-old French or Italian bread and a little brandy for pizzazz. This is a very rich version. Serve it for Sunday brunch with sausages and, also à la New Orleans, with lots of cane syrup.

4 large eggs
2 cups milk
¼ teaspoon vanilla extract
1 tablespoon brandy
1 tablespoon granulated sugar
8 slices day-old French or Italian
    bread, cut 1 inch thick at a
    45-degree angle
4 tablespoons (½ stick) unsalted butter
Confectioners' sugar, for dusting

1. Preheat the oven to 200°F, and place four plates in it to warm.

2. In a shallow bowl, beat the eggs, milk, vanilla, brandy, and granulated sugar together until well blended. Place 4 slices of the bread in the milk and egg mixture and let them soak for a few minutes, turning them if necessary to make sure they are soaked through. Meanwhile, melt 2 tablespoons of the butter in a large skillet over medium heat.

3. Using your hands, pick up the bread slices one at a time, allowing the excess liquid to drain off into the bowl, and place them in the skillet. Fry them in the butter until golden brown on both sides, 4 or 5 minutes total. Divide the slices among the plates in the oven, and repeat the process with the remaining bread slices and butter. Serve hot, dusted with confectioners' sugar.

BREAKFAST PANCAKES

SERVES 4

Hotcakes like these are served in countless diners across the country as part of a hearty breakfast. On Shrove Tuesday, Episcopal and Catholic parishes offer pancake suppers as the last feast before Lent. I like these, made with buttermilk; you can add sliced bananas and chopped pecans for a southern touch. If you don't have a well-seasoned griddle or skillet, you may need to add a little butter to the pan. Serve with bacon or sausages and plenty of cane, maple, or sorghum syrup. Some people like extra butter as well.

2 cups all-purpose flour
1 teaspoon baking soda
½ teaspoon salt
2 large eggs, separated
2 cups buttermilk
2 tablespoons unsalted butter, melted

1. Preheat the oven to 200°F and place four plates in it to warm.

2. Sift the flour, baking soda, and salt together into a large mixing bowl. In another bowl, beat the egg yolks into the buttermilk. Pour the liquid into the dry ingredients, mixing well. Stir in the melted butter.

3. Preheat a well-seasoned griddle or skillet over medium-high heat.

4. Beat the egg whites until they hold soft peaks, then fold them into the batter. Using a ladle, pour the batter onto the hot griddle to form pancakes about 4 inches wide and ¼ inch thick. Cook until the tops of the pancakes begin to bubble and have started to brown on the edges. Flip the pancakes and cook until browned on the second side. Transfer the pancakes to the warmed plates in the oven, and continue cooking the rest of the batter. Serve immediately.

GRIDDLE CAKES

Every culture has its version of griddle cakes, from the paper-thin *mu xi* flour pancakes of China to the creamy *palacsinta* of Hungary. Batters poured onto hot surfaces were certainly among man's first breads. These are the three most common: thick American breakfast pancakes, airy French crêpes suitable for late-night suppers and desserts, and blini, the small yeast-raised buckwheat pancakes that are served with sour cream and caviar in Russia.

CREPES

MAKES 12 TO 15 CREPES

There is no leavening in these thin French pancakes, and they can be stuffed and rolled with any number of fillings, both sweet and savory. I like to add a few crushed pecans to the batter and serve them with rich duck dishes. Filled with sweetened ricotta or cottage cheese and served with jam, crêpes become blintzes. The famous dish, crêpes Suzette, is made of crêpes that are spread with orange-flavored butter, fried a second time, and then flamed with brandy and orange liqueur.

If you have a well-seasoned crêpe pan, by all means use it; if not, here's the one time I recommend a thin nonstick pan. It should have sloped sides for easy turning of the crêpes.

1 cup all-purpose flour
Pinch of salt
2 large eggs
1 cup milk
2 tablespoons unsalted butter, melted
2 tablespoons clarified butter (page 8)

1. Sift the flour and salt together into a medium bowl, and make a well in the center. Add the eggs and about ⅓ cup of the milk to the well, and stir with a wire whisk, gradually adding the remaining milk until it is all incorporated into the batter. Add the melted butter and stir until perfectly smooth. There should be no lumps.

2. Preheat the oven to 200°F and place a plate in it to warm.

3. Heat a small amount of the clarified butter in an omelet or crêpe pan over medium-high heat until it is very hot but not smoking. Swirl it around to completely coat the bottom and partway up the sides, then pour off any excess. Using a ladle, quickly pour about 2 tablespoons of the batter into the hot pan and swirl it around to coat the bottom of the pan. Cook until the edges just begin to pull away from the pan, 1 or 2 minutes. Then, carefully flip the crêpe over by loosening the edges with a spatula, then carefully peeling up the rest of the crêpe with your fingers and cook until done, a matter of seconds. Transfer the crêpe to the warm plate in the oven, and repeat the process with the rest of the batter, adding clarified butter to the pan only as needed. Serve the warm crêpes however you wish.

BLINI

MAKES ABOUT 18 BLINI

Blini are small buckwheat pancakes that are traditionally served with caviar and sour cream. This recipe will serve six as an appetizer. Make the batter before dinner, then start cooking the blini as your guests are seated at the table. Serve them piping hot, with chilled caviar and room-temperature sour cream.

1 teaspoon active dry yeast

1 cup milk, warmed

1 to 1¼ cups buckwheat flour

2 large eggs, separated

1 teaspoon salt

1 teaspoon sugar

1 tablespoon unsalted butter, melted

2 to 3 tablespoons clarified butter
(page 8)

1 cup sour cream, at room temperature

2 ounces caviar of choice, chilled

1. Stir the yeast into ½ cup of the milk in a medium bowl. Then stir in about ½ cup of the flour to make a stiff dough. Cover with plastic wrap and let rise until doubled in bulk, 2 to 3 hours.

2. In another bowl, beat the egg yolks with the salt, sugar, and melted butter. Add the remaining ½ cup milk and mix well. Then pour the mixture onto the dough and mix well. Add ½ cup of the remaining flour and beat with a wooden spoon until you have a smooth batter. If it seems too thin, add a little more flour.

3. Beat the egg whites until they hold stiff peaks but are not dry, and fold them into the batter. Cover the bowl and let stand for about 30 minutes.

4. When you are ready to serve the blini, preheat the oven to 200°F and place six appetizer plates in it to warm.

5. Pour a little of the clarified butter into a well-seasoned griddle or skillet and place it over medium-high heat. Pour small ladlefuls of batter onto the hot griddle, forming 3-inch blini. Cook until browned on both sides, 1 to 2 minutes on each side. Place the blini on the warmed plates in the oven while you prepare the rest. Serve immediately, spooning a dollop of sour cream onto each blini and topping the cream with a teaspoon of caviar.

FRESH CORN CAKES

MAKES 12 CORN CAKES

Y ou can top these fresh corn pancakes with your favorite stewed meats or serve them alongside a roast and greens. This is just one of the many types of cornbreads offered in the Deep South. If you are serving spicy food over the corn cakes, omit the jalapeño.

2 cups corn kernels, either blanched fresh kernels (see Notes) or thawed frozen kernels

½ cup finely chopped scallions, including some of the green tops

½ cup finely chopped red bell pepper or jarred pimiento (see Notes)

1 jalapeño pepper, seeded, deribbed, and finely chopped (optional)

½ teaspoon ground cumin

1 teaspoon salt

2 large eggs, separated

½ cup heavy (or whipping) cream

2 tablespoons unsalted butter, melted

2 cups corn flour (see box, page 41) or masa harina (see Sources, page 189)

2 tablespoons unsalted butter

1. In a large mixing bowl, combine the corn, scallions, bell pepper, jalapeño, cumin, and salt.

2. In a small bowl, mix the egg yolks with the cream. Add this to the vegetables, stirring well. Add the melted butter and mix well. Then mix in the corn flour.

3. Beat the egg whites until they hold soft peaks, then fold them into the corn mixture. Melt the 2 tablespoons butter in a large skillet over medium heat. Scoop up a large tablespoonful of the batter, place it in the skillet, and flatten it out to form a pancake about 3 inches across and ½ inch thick. Add as many more as you can without crowding. Fry until golden brown, about 2 or 3 minutes on each side. Transfer the corn cakes to a plate and keep them warm in a low (200°F) oven while you fry the remaining cakes.

Notes: To blanch fresh corn, simply place freshly shucked ears in a pot of boiling water, cover, and turn off the heat. Let them sit for about 10 minutes in the water. You can use roasted red peppers in this recipe if you prefer. Follow the directions for roasting on page 173, or use bottled roasted peppers.

BASIC GRITS CAKES

MAKES 8 GRITS CAKES

Southerners love to fry, and throughout the region you find fritters made from left-over rice, fish, chicken, beans, and grits. These grits cakes are delicious served alongside roast chicken or lamb in lieu of potatoes, but they're also good when topped with an elegant sauce such as Sautéed Oysters (see Index).

Basic Grits (page 186)
2 large eggs
2 tablespoons heavy (or whipping)
  cream
2 teaspoons water
¼ cup all-purpose flour, cornmeal,
  corn flour (see box, page 41), or
  fine dry bread crumbs
Peanut oil for frying

1. Grease a 9-inch round cake pan.

2. As soon as the grits are cooked, place one of the eggs in a medium-size mixing bowl, add the cream, and stir well to combine. Quickly add a few tablespoons of the grits to the mixture, beating well with a whisk so the egg doesn't curdle. Then transfer the mixture to the pot containing the remaining grits, and whisk together well.

3. Pour the grits into the cake pan and cool to room temperature. Refrigerate until firm.

4. When you are ready to cook the grits cakes, preheat the oven to 200°F. Place a wire rack on a baking sheet and set it in the oven.

5. Remove the grits from the refrigerator and invert the pan onto a cutting surface. The grits will come out in one big cake.

6. Beat the remaining egg with the water in a shallow bowl. Place the flour in another shallow bowl. Cut the grits into eight wedges and gently dip each one into the beaten egg and then into the flour.

7. The grits cakes can be deep-fried, but pan-frying is less messy, so that is how I make them. To pan-fry them, pour oil to a depth of ¾ inch in a heavy skillet and place it over medium-high heat. When the oil is hot, add as many grits cakes as will fit comfortably in the skillet and fry until golden brown, about 3 minutes on each side. Place the cooked cakes on the rack in the oven to drain and stay warm while you fry the rest of the cakes. Serve warm.

SOPAIPILLAS

MAKES 8 TO 10 SOPAIPILLAS

Albuquerque, New Mexico, claims this fried bread as its own. It is related to both Navajo fry breads and Spanish *buñuelos* (fritters). The distinctive American touch is the baking powder. These southwestern "sofa pillows" are served a number of ways, but most often a corner is bitten off and the warm bread is filled with honey butter. Amazingly, these sweet treats are a good accompaniment to chili.

I suppose you could use vegetable shortening instead of lard for these, but it's not authentic, so I won't recommend it.

1¼ cups all-purpose flour
1 teaspoon baking powder
½ teaspoon salt
2 tablespoons lard
⅜ cup warm water
8 tablespoons (1 stick) unsalted butter
5 tablespoons honey
½ teaspoon ground cinnamon
Peanut oil for deep-frying

1. Sift the flour, baking powder, and salt together into a large mixing bowl with sloping sides. Using a pastry blender or two knives, cut in the lard until it is evenly incorporated. Pour the warm water into the bowl all at once, and stir with a wooden spoon until the dough can be gathered into a ball.

2. Dust a work surface and a rolling pin with flour. Place the dough on the surface. Work the dough with your fingertips, turning it a quarter-turn, folding it over on itself, patting it out, then turning it a quarter-turn again.

Repeat until the dough is no longer sticky, but do not overwork it; a maximum of ten folds should do it. Cover the dough with a damp tea towel and let it rest for 15 minutes.

3. Meanwhile, combine the butter, honey, and cinnamon in a small saucepan and place it over low heat. Heat, stirring, until the butter melts and the mixture is thoroughly blended. Remove from the heat and set aside, covered, to keep warm.

4. Preheat the oven to 200°F. Place a wire rack on a baking sheet and set it in the oven.

5. Pour oil into a stockpot or Dutch oven to a depth of 3 inches, place it over medium-high heat, and heat it to 400°F.

6. While the oil is heating, divide the dough in half, and re-cover the half you aren't using. Roll the dough out to form a circle about ⅛ inch thick. Cut the circle into four or five wedges.

7. When the oil reaches 400°F, fry the wedges, two or three at a time, turning them as soon as they are browned and puffed on the bottom, 30 seconds to 1 minute. As soon as the second side is puffed and browned, transfer them to the wire rack to drain and stay warm while you fry the rest of the sopaipillas, using the same method for the second half of the dough. Serve the sopaipillas warm or at room temperature, with the honey butter.

NICK MALGIERI'S PANELLE

MAKES 16 TO 24 FRITTERS

Nick Malgieri, who sent me this recipe, is a baker and a teacher and the author of several wonderful books, *How to Bake* being his most recent. These Sicilian chickpea-flour fritters are a specialty of Palermo's great old *focaccierie*—informal establishments where different types of focaccia and fried foods are available throughout the day and evening. When I lived in Genoa, a city with strong Arabic influences, the *farinata* shop was where you found foods made with chickpeas. Farinata is baked in a hot wood-fired oven; panelle is essentially a fried version of the same dish.

You need to make the panelle paste at least an hour ahead of time. If you like, you can prepare it in advance and store it, well wrapped, in the refrigerator for several days.

Vegetable oil

3 cups water

1 teaspoon salt

2 cups chickpea flour (see box)

1. Coat a 10½ × 15½-inch jelly-roll pan with oil; then line it with plastic wrap. Coat the wrap with oil.

2. Place the water and salt in a saucepan and sift in the chickpea flour a little at a time, whisking constantly to avoid lumps. Cook over low heat, stirring constantly, until very thick, 5 to 10 minutes.

3. Scrape the paste into the prepared pan and spread it out evenly. It should be about ¼ inch thick. Allow it to cool for at least 1 hour.

4. When you are ready to cook the panelle, pour oil to a depth of 2 inches in a Dutch oven or stockpot, place it over medium heat, and heat it to 350°F.

5. While the oil is heating, cut the paste into rectangles, then cut some of the rectangles on the diagonal into triangles.

6. When the oil reaches 350°F, remove the panelle from the pan (making sure no plastic wrap is stuck to them), and fry them in the hot

CHICKPEA FLOUR

Chickpeas, or garbanzo beans, are used extensively in the cooking of the Mediterranean and the Middle East. In India, the beans are roasted and ground into *besan*, a flour that is used in both flatbreads and fritters. The flour is also popular in Sicily and southern Italy, where Arabic influences are most evident in the kitchen. Look for chickpea flour in Indian and Italian markets or in health-food stores.

oil until they are light golden, about 3 minutes. They will not color deeply; do not overcook them. Drain them on paper towels and serve immediately as an hors d'oeuvre or snack.

CHICKPEA FRITTERS WITH SORREL

MAKES 12 TO 16 FRITTERS

In India, this light fritter batter is used with a variety of leafy greens and whole herb leaves. The fritters are called *pakoras*. Pieces of steamed cauliflower and eggplant can also be dipped in the batter. I like to use small leaves of sour French sorrel; I serve these with a creamy sorrel soup or with Cucumber and Yogurt Salad (see Index). This batter needs a resting period of about 2 hours, so plan accordingly.

1¼ cups chickpea flour (see box, page 20)
1 teaspoon salt
1 teaspoon baking powder
1½ teaspoons ground cumin
Pinch of sugar
¾ cup water, more or less
Peanut oil for frying
12 to 16 very young sorrel or spinach leaves (or large basil leaves), without heavy stems or ribs, rinsed and patted perfectly dry

1. Combine the chickpea flour, salt, baking powder, cumin, and sugar in a medium-size bowl. Add the water slowly, stirring constantly until you have a thick pancake batter. Do not overmix. Cover the bowl and let the batter rest at room temperature for 2 hours.

2. Place a wire rack on a baking sheet and set it near the stove. Pour oil to a depth of 2 or 3 inches in a stockpot or Dutch oven, place it over medium-high heat, and heat it to 375°F. Uncover the batter and thin it with a little water if it seems too thick.

3. When the oil has reached 375°F, drag the leaves, one at a time, through the batter; you want about 1 tablespoon of batter coating each leaf. Drop the coated leaves, one by one, into the hot oil. Maintain the oil temperature between 365° and 375°F, and do not crowd the pot. Remove the fritters with tongs or a wire mesh strainer, and place them on the wire rack. Serve immediately.

CROUTONS

MAKES ABOUT 2 CUPS

Americans seem to think that croutons go mainly with salads (and they certainly can), but in France they're served with many heavily sauced foods and with creamy soups. In southern Italy, cooks fry big cubes of day-old bread in olive oil, then stir the croutons into a purée of fava beans. I like them with my recipe for Bitter Greens (see Index).

You can store leftover croutons for about 24 hours if you wrap them well in aluminum foil. Reheat them in the foil (at 350°F) when you are ready to serve them, to make sure they are crisp. Croutons can be made by brushing bread slices with fat and then grilling or baking them, but the classic French method makes a crisp, buttery version. Use fresh bread for this recipe, not stale.

4 slices dense, homestyle white bread, sliced ¼ inch thick
8 tablespoons (1 stick) unsalted butter, clarified (page 8)

Trim the crusts off the bread, and dice the bread. Pour clarified butter to a depth of ¼ inch in a sauté pan, and place it over medium-high heat. Cover three quarters of the bottom of the pan with croutons and sauté them, stirring constantly, until they are golden brown all over, about 4 minutes. Drain on paper towels. Repeat the procedure with any remaining bread cubes.

TWO CRISPY TREATS

When polled about the favorite flavor in their restaurants, American chefs answer, "Crunch!" Crispiness is a texture, of course, but it's the most desirable one on today's menus. These two classic fried breads—croutons and tortilla chips—provide crunch in restaurants from San Diego to Boston. They're easy to make and are infinitely superior to store-bought (though you can use store-bought bread and tortillas). I like to make them before I go to a dinner party, package them in a nice tin, and offer them to my host.

TORTILLA CHIPS

SERVES 6 TO 8

Most of us have eaten our weight several times over in chips. Many restaurants that specialize in pub food serve homemade potato chips, but few serve homemade tortilla chips, which are infinitely superior to store-bought. They are also incredibly simple to make.

When I'm invited to a potluck dinner in the summer, I'll often ask if I can bring chips and salsa. I make a big bowl of salsa from vine-ripened tomatoes, then fry a batch of these chips. I place them in a large roasting pan and keep them in a warm oven until it's time to go to the party. Just before leaving, I cover the pot with foil so they're still warm when I arrive, ready to start the festivities.

You don't have to bother to make or find fresh tortillas—the packaged ones in your grocer's refrigerated section are actually better for frying because they are thinner and drier. Look for ones that are labeled "stone ground"—they'll be the tastiest. A six- to eight-ounce package of 6-inch corn tortillas yields chips for about three people.

Though I drain most fried foods on wire racks, I place chips on paper towels because their crescent shape tends to hold oil. It's easier to position them to drain on the towels. If you sprinkle these with grated cheese and chopped chiles while they're still warm, you'll have instant nachos.

2 packages (8 ounces each) 6-inch
corn tortillas
Peanut or corn oil for frying
Salt, for serving

1. Cut the tortillas into six to eight wedges each, and spread them out on paper towels to dry, about 1 hour.

2. If the chips aren't going to be eaten immediately, preheat the oven to 200°F and place a baking sheet in it.

3. Pour oil to a depth of 2 inches in a stockpot, place it over medium-high heat, and heat it to 375°F. Line a baking sheet with paper towels and set aside.

4. Place the chips one at a time on the surface of the hot oil, adding just enough to the

pot so they can fry without being crowded. Cook for about 30 seconds, or until they just begin to blush with color. Then turn them over to fry on the other side until lightly colored, 30 seconds more. (If you let them color completely, they will be overcooked.) Remove the chips immediately with a wire mesh strainer or tongs, draining as much oil back into the pot as possible. Place the hot chips on the paper-towel-lined baking sheet.

5. Allow the oil to return to 375°F before adding another batch of chips. Remove the first batch from the paper towels and place them in the warm oven while you continue frying. Use clean paper towels for each batch. Repeat until all the chips have been fried.

6. Salt the chips right before serving. Serve warm, with Salsa (page 171).

CHAPTER 3

EGGS AND CHEESE

This chapter features eggs and cheese front and center, but they also appear throughout the book as important ingredients for frying. You can fry just about any cheese by coating it first with flour, then with egg, and lastly with bread crumbs before dropping it into hot oil. The recipe is infinitely variable by changing cheeses and seasonings. Nearly every country has its own version of a fried cheese turnover, although I've only included the Italian calzone. While living in France and Italy, I became spoiled by the dizzying variety of cheeses available in Europe. Most of these cheese recipes are, not surprisingly, Italian in origin. But Mexico's stuffed peppers, chiles relleños, are one of my favorite dishes, and I've included the recipe here as well.

Most of these dishes I serve as finger food to pass with a glass of wine before dinner, but stuffed peppers make a wonderful main course, as do the Scots Eggs. Incidentally, I had always thought this dish of hard-cooked eggs encased in sausage—then fried—a peculiarity of the British Isles until I found a virtually identical recipe from China! I guess that just goes to prove what I've always suspected: No one owns recipes, especially not international favorites like these.

FRIED EGG SALAD

SERVES 4

This is not a salad made with fried eggs, but rather a croquette made of egg salad and served as an hors d'oeuvre. You can use leftover egg salad (or potato salad, for that matter) or you can make it up fresh for this dish. Olives or pickles can be added to the salad if you wish. It will have to chill for several hours, so plan accordingly.

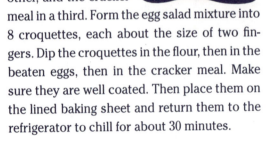

6 large hard-cooked eggs, peeled and
    chopped
1 tablespoon grated onion
1 teaspoon salt
2 teaspoons prepared mustard
Freshly ground black pepper,
    to taste
2 tablespoons finely chopped celery
½ cup mayonnaise
1 tablespoon finely chopped pickles
    or olives (optional)
½ cup all-purpose flour
2 large eggs, beaten
1 cup cracker meal
Peanut oil for frying

1. Make the egg salad by combining the eggs, onion, salt, mustard, pepper, celery, mayonnaise, and pickles or olives, if using, in a medium-size bowl. Toss together well, then cover and chill for several hours in the refrigerator.

2. About 1 hour before you plan to serve the croquettes, remove the egg salad from the refrigerator. Line a baking sheet with wax paper or parchment.

3. Place the flour in a shallow bowl, the beaten eggs in another, and the cracker meal in a third. Form the egg salad mixture into 8 croquettes, each about the size of two fingers. Dip the croquettes in the flour, then in the beaten eggs, then in the cracker meal. Make sure they are well coated. Then place them on the lined baking sheet and return them to the refrigerator to chill for about 30 minutes.

4. When you are ready to cook the croquettes, pour peanut oil to a depth of 1 inch in a large skillet, place it over medium-high heat, and heat it to 375°F. Place a wire rack on a baking sheet and set it near the stove. Remove the chilled croquettes from the refrigerator.

5. When the oil reaches 375°F, fry the croquettes, without crowding the skillet, until golden brown, about 2 minutes on each side. (Do this in batches if necessary.) Transfer them to the wire rack to drain, and serve them immediately.

SCOTS EGGS

SERVES 6

This Scottish dish of deep-fried eggs wrapped in forcemeat appears in *The Cook and Housewife's Manual* by Meg Dods, first published in Edinburgh in 1826. Miss Dods made a highly seasoned forcemeat of grated ham, anchovies, and bread crumbs. She served the dish hot, with a gravy. Today's versions often call for prepared pork sausage as the forcemeat; most writers recommend the eggs as picnic fare. I, too, use sausage, but I prefer to serve them hot as per Miss Dods, with a classic soubise—an onion-infused cream sauce. Serve this with hot grits, followed by fresh fruit, as a breakfast or supper dish.

Nevertheless, these eggs *are* delightful on a picnic. If you plan to serve them at room temperature, without a sauce, be sure to hard-cook the eggs. When serving them hot, I prefer that the yolk be as uncooked as possible.

7 large eggs
1 cup Soubise (optional; page 168)
Peanut oil for deep-frying
1 pound bulk pork sausage
⅓ cup dry bread crumbs

1. In a small saucepan, cover 6 eggs with cold water and bring to a boil. Immediately cover the pan, remove it from the heat, and allow to sit for 5 minutes, if you will be serving the eggs hot (the yolks won't be totally firm). Let the eggs sit for 10 minutes, if you will be serving them cold (the yolks will be hard-cooked).

2. Meanwhile, prepare a pan of ice water. Remove the eggs from the hot water with a slotted spoon and plunge them into the ice water. Leave them for about 1 minute, until

cooled. Then return them to the pot of hot water, using the slotted spoon. Immediately transfer them again to the ice water. Remove the eggs one at a time to peel. Gently tap each egg all over so that the entire surface of the

shell is crackled. Peel the eggs very carefully under cold running water, starting at the large end. Eggs that are not hard-cooked will be very delicate, but they can be peeled with care. Use a thin-bladed paring knife to slip under the shell if necessary. Set the 6 peeled eggs aside.

3. If you will be serving the eggs hot, make the Soubise.

4. Pour oil to a depth of 3 to 4 inches in a stock pot or Dutch oven, place it over medium-high heat, and heat it to 375°F.

5. While the oil is heating, roll the sausage out between two pieces of wax paper or parchment so that it is about ¼ inch thick. Remove the top piece of wax paper and, using a sharp knife, cut the sausage into six equal portions, cutting through the bottom layer of wax paper. Place one of the pieces of sausage in the palm of your hand, remove the wax paper,

and place a cooked egg on the sausage. Wrap the sausage meat around the egg. Then use both hands to gently and evenly pat the meat around the egg. Repeat with the remaining eggs and sausage.

6. Lightly beat the remaining egg in a shallow dish or bowl. Place the bread crumbs on a plate. Dip each sausage-wrapped egg in the egg wash, then roll it in the bread crumbs.

7. Place a wire rack on a baking sheet. Check that the oil has reached 375°F. Fry 2 or 3 eggs at a time (do not crowd the pot) until golden brown all over, 3 to 4 minutes. Drain the eggs on the wire rack. If you are serving them cold, allow them to cool completely and then wrap each one in aluminum foil to take on a picnic. If you are serving the dish hot, slice each egg in half and place them, one half facing up and the other down, on warmed plates. Drizzle with the Soubise, and serve immediately.

GOAT CHEESE GRITS CROUTONS

MAKES 60 TO 120 CROUTONS, ENOUGH TO GARNISH 6 TO 12 SALADS

This recipe comes from Michael McNally, chef-owner of Philadelphia's London Grill. I've had the pleasure of working with Michael several times in his restaurant and can honestly say I've never met a more even-tempered or talented chef. His cross-cultural recipes never seem contrived because he never sacrifices the integrity of the fine ingredients he seeks out.

These croutons were developed for a salad that Michael makes with Szechuan duck and summer beans, but I serve them with all sorts of dishes. They're good with any greens, fresh or cooked.

4 cups homemade chicken stock or canned broth
1 cup stone-ground whole-grain grits (see Sources, page 189)
½ teaspoon salt (optional)
½ cup soft goat cheese
Peanut oil for deep-frying
1 large egg yolk
1 tablespoon water

1. Pour the stock into a large saucepan and bring it to a boil. Stir in the grits, and add the salt if the stock is not salty. Simmer, stirring often, until the grits are soft and creamy, 20 to 30 minutes. Stir the cheese into the grits. Then pour the mixture into an 8-inch square baking pan and chill it in the refrigerator until firm, at least 1 hour.

2. Invert the baking pan over a cutting surface; the chilled grits should come out whole. Cut the grits into little squares (½ to 1 inch); roll each little square to form a ball.

3. Pour oil to a depth of 3 inches in a stockpot or Dutch oven, place it over medium-high heat, and heat it to 365°F. Line a baking sheet with paper towels and set it near the stove.

4. Beat the egg yolk with the water in a shallow bowl. Dip each ball into the egg mixture, and fry them until golden, 1 to 2 minutes. Don't crowd the pot, and remove the croutons in the order in which they were put in the pot. Drain the croutons on the prepared baking sheet.

CRISPY CHEESE FRITTERS

MAKES ABOUT 24 FRITTERS

These European fritters can be made with your choice of cheeses. You'll need to start by making a Béchamel Sauce (basic white sauce), but the recipe is quick and simple. Pass these fritters while they're still hot.

Béchamel Sauce (page 169;
   see step 1)
1½ cups grated Gruyère, Gouda,
   Edam, or Cheddar cheese
3 large eggs, separated
Peanut oil for deep-frying

1. Make the Béchamel Sauce, stirring in the grated cheese as soon as the sauce is smooth and thick. Remove from the heat, allow to cool a little, and then beat in the egg yolks.

2. Pour oil to a depth of 3 inches in a stock-pot or Dutch oven, place it over medium-high heat, and heat it to 375°F. Place a wire rack on a baking sheet, and set it near the stove.

3. While the oil is heating, beat the egg whites until they hold stiff peaks but are not dry. Fold them into the fritter batter.

4. When the oil reaches 375°F, drop the batter by heaping teaspoons into the oil, frying them until they are golden brown, about 3 minutes. Be sure to maintain the temperature between 365° and 375°F, and do not crowd the pot. Transfer the fritters to the wire rack to drain, and finish the frying. Serve the fritters immediately.

FRIED CALZONE

**MAKES ABOUT 36 CALZONE;
SERVES 8 TO 10 AS AN APPETIZER**

Most of the calzone we see in this country are baked, but in Naples, where they originated, these pizza turnovers are just as likely to be deep-fried. You can stuff them as you like, the way you might top a pizza, but the simple little prosciutto-and-cheese-filled ones are a classic combination. You can substitute country ham, salami, or pepperoni for the prosciutto. A little bit of dried herbs, such as oregano or marjoram, or a mix such as herbes de Provence or Italian seasoning, adds a Mediterranean flavor.

1 teaspoon active dry yeast
1¼ cups warm water
Pinch of sugar
1 pound all-purpose flour
    (about 3¼ cups)
1½ teaspoons salt
2 tablespoons fruity olive oil
½ pound prosciutto, thinly sliced
    and cut into bite-size pieces
½ pound mozzarella cheese, grated
Freshly ground black pepper, to taste
Dried herbs (see headnote), to taste
Peanut oil for deep-frying

1. Dissolve the yeast in ¼ cup of the warm water in a medium-size bowl. Sprinkle with the sugar and set aside for about 10 minutes. It should be creamy and bubbly. Then add 1 cup of the flour, and mix until smooth.

2. Warm a large mixing bowl by swirling some boiling water around in it. Pour out the water and thoroughly dry the bowl. Combine the remaining flour and the salt in it. Make a well in the center, and pour in the yeast mixture. Add 2 teaspoons of the olive oil, and mix well. Gradually add the remaining 1 cup warm water, and continue to mix until the dough forms a ball and no longer sticks to your hands or to the bowl. Place the dough on a lightly floured surface and knead until it is very smooth and shiny, about 10 minutes.

3. Wipe out the large mixing bowl and sprinkle it with flour. Form the dough into a ball and place it in the bowl. With a razor blade, cut an "X" in the top of the dough. Sprinkle it with a little more flour, and place the entire bowl inside a large plastic bag, loosely sealed. Set aside to rise until doubled in size, about 2 hours.

4. Lightly flour a work surface and a rolling pin. Punch the dough down and turn it out onto the floured surface. Roll it out as thin as you can, about ¹⁄₁₆ inch thick. Using a pizza

wheel or a small thin knife, cut out about thirty-six 4-inch rounds of dough. Place a piece of prosciutto and a little cheese on each round, then sprinkle each with a little pepper and herbs and a few drops of the remaining olive oil. Fold the rounds in half, press the edges together, and seal them with the tines of a fork.

5. Pour oil to a depth of 3 inches in a stockpot or Dutch oven, place it over medium-high heat, and heat it to 375°F. Line a baking sheet with paper towels and place it near the stove.

6. When the oil reaches 375°F, place the calzone, two or three at a time, in the oil and fry until golden brown all over, 2 to 3 minutes on each side. Remove the calzone with tongs or a wire mesh strainer, allowing excess oil to drain back into the pot before placing them on the paper towels to drain further. Pat them dry, if necessary, and serve immediately.

PARMESAN PUFFS

MAKES ABOUT 12 PUFFS

These are the easiest fritters to make, but you must prepare them at the very last moment. They are a delicious appetizer, but they can accompany salads, stews, and cooked greens as well.

Peanut oil for deep-frying
3 large egg whites
1 cup freshly grated Parmesan cheese
¼ teaspoon cayenne pepper

1. Pour oil to a depth of 2 inches in a stockpot or Dutch oven, place it over medium-high heat, and heat it to 375°F. Place a wire rack on a baking sheet and set it near the stove.

2. While the oil is heating, beat the egg whites until they hold stiff peaks. Sprinkle about ⅔ cup of the cheese and the cayenne over the whites, and fold in. Place the remaining cheese on a piece of wax paper and dust your hands with it.

3. When the oil reaches 375°F, quickly roll small balls of the egg white mixture between your palms and carefully drop them into the oil. Do not crowd the pot. Remove the puffs as soon as they are lightly browned all over, about 2 minutes. Transfer them to the wire rack to drain, and sprinkle with more cheese if desired. Serve immediately.

FRIED MOZZARELLA

MAKES ABOUT 30 FRITTERS

This is another of the innumerable Italian recipes for fritters that call for a flour, egg, and bread-crumb coating. You can fry any good melting cheese this way, but mozzarella is especially good because when you bite into it, it stretches into strings that will hold a sauce. You can use the anchovy and caper sauce that is served with the Mozzarella Sandwiches on page 34 (step 1), or you can offer any of the red sauces in the Go-Withs chapter. Of course, these fritters are perfectly delicious without a sauce.

Serve these bite-size cubes as an appetizer at a party. You'll have to get started about an hour before you plan to serve them.

½ cup all-purpose flour
2 large eggs
½ cup fine dry bread crumbs
1 pound mozzarella cheese, cut
    into 1-inch cubes
Peanut oil for deep-frying

1. Line a baking sheet with wax paper or parchment. Place the flour in a heavy paper bag. Beat the eggs in a shallow bowl, and place the bread crumbs in another bowl.

2. Add the cheese cubes, a few at a time, to the flour and shake the bag to coat them. Dip the floured cubes in the egg, allowing any excess to drain off, and then roll them in the crumbs, making sure the cheese is totally covered. Place the coated cheese cubes on the prepared baking sheet, and chill in the refrigerator for at least 30 minutes or up to 2 hours.

3. Pour oil to a depth of 3 or 4 inches in a stockpot or Dutch oven, place it over medium-high heat, and heat it to 375°F. Remove the cheese cubes from the refrigerator. Place a wire rack over a baking sheet and set it near the stove.

4. When the oil reaches 375°F, fry the cubes, without crowding the pot, until they are golden brown all over, 1 to 3 minutes; the time will vary greatly according to how cold the cheese is. Maintain the oil temperature between 365° and 375°F. Remove the fritters from the oil, using tongs or a wire mesh strainer, allowing the excess oil to drain back into the pot. Place them on the wire rack and continue with the frying until they are all cooked. Serve warm, with or without a sauce (see headnote).

MOZZARELLA SANDWICHES

SERVES 4 TO 6

This famous southern Italian dish, *mozzarella in carrozza* (mozzarella in a carriage), is traditionally served as an appetizer with an anchovy sauce. You can serve it with Tomato Sauce (see Index) if you prefer. You needn't use the expensive water-buffalo mozzarella, but do try to find fresh water-packed mozzarella in half-pound balls.

1 tin (2 ounces) flat anchovy fillets
    in oil, drained
½ cup loosely packed fresh parsley
    leaves
1 clove garlic
1 tablespoon capers, rinsed and drained
1 tablespoon fresh lemon juice
½ cup olive oil
1 loaf homestyle white bread
    (about 1 pound), cut into
    ¼-inch-thick slices
½ pound fresh mozzarella, thinly sliced
Olive oil for frying
3 tablespoons milk
2 large eggs
½ teaspoon salt
1 cup fine dry bread
    crumbs

1. Place the anchovies, parsley, garlic, and capers on a cutting surface and chop with a heavy knife until evenly minced and mixed. Place the mixture in a small saucepan, add the lemon juice and ½ cup olive oil, and place over low heat for about 5 minutes, stirring occasionally. Keep warm while preparing the rest of the recipe.

2. Use a cookie or biscuit cutter to cut 3-inch rounds, with no crusts, from the bread. Sandwich each slice of mozzarella between 2 rounds of bread, making sure no cheese protrudes from the edges of the sandwiches.

3. Pour olive oil to a depth of 1 inch in a large skillet, place it over medium-high heat, and heat it to 375°F. Preheat the oven to 200°F. Place a wire rack on a baking sheet and set it in the oven.

4. Beat the milk, eggs, and salt together in a shallow bowl. Place the bread crumbs on a sheet of wax paper. Submerge each sandwich in the egg mixture to soak both sides. Then drain it well and roll it *along its edge* in the

crumbs. Then place the flat sides down in the crumbs as well, to make sure the sandwich is well coated.

5. When the oil reaches 375°F, fry each sandwich until golden brown, about 2 minutes on each side. Do not crowd the pot; maintain a temperature between 365° and 375°F. Remove each sandwich from the oil with tongs, holding it over the pot to drain off excess oil; then place it on the wire rack to drain and stay warm while you fry the remaining sandwiches. Serve immediately, passing the anchovy sauce in a gravy boat.

RISOTTO CROQUETTES

MAKES ABOUT 24 CROQUETTES; SERVES 8 AS AN APPETIZER

Cheesy risotto is molded around a mozzarella center and deep-fried to make these balls called *supplì* or *arancini* (little oranges) in Italy. For this simple risotto, you needn't stand over the pot, stirring and stirring. If you make the risotto the night before, you can chill it in the refrigerator and it will be much easier to form into balls.

2 tablespoons butter
¼ cup finely chopped onion
1 cup short-grain rice, preferably
    Arborio
3 cups homemade chicken stock,
    canned chicken broth, or water,
    or more as needed
1 teaspoon salt, or to taste
¼ cup grated Parmesan cheese
2 large eggs
¾ cup fine dry bread crumbs
¼ pound mozzarella cheese, cut
    into ½-inch cubes
Peanut oil for deep-frying

1. Several hours or the night before you plan to serve the croquettes, make the risotto: Melt the butter in a heavy saucepan over medium heat. Add the onion and cook, stirring, until it has softened, 5 to 10 minutes. Then stir in the rice, the stock, and the salt (if you are using canned broth, taste it for saltiness and adjust accordingly). Raise the heat and bring to a boil. Immediately reduce the heat, cover, and simmer until the liquid is absorbed and the rice is tender, 10 to 20 minutes. Lift the lid and stir the rice occasionally. If the rice is not tender but the liquid has been absorbed, add more liquid and cook, stirring constantly, until it softens.

2. Remove the rice from the heat and stir in the Parmesan. Then transfer the mixture to a bowl and let it cool to room temperature.

3. Lightly beat the eggs and stir them into the cooled rice. Cover the bowl and place it in the refrigerator to chill, at least 2 hours.

4. About 1 hour before serving time, remove the risotto from the refrigerator. Line a baking sheet with wax paper or parchment. Place the bread crumbs in a shallow bowl. Wet your hands with water, scoop up a tablespoon of risotto, and pat it into one of your palms. Place a cube of mozzarella on the risotto. Then scoop up another tablespoon of risotto and place it over the cheese. Press the mixture into a ball, making sure that the mozzarella is covered. Roll the ball in the bread crumbs, coating it well. Place the croquette on the paper-lined baking sheet, and repeat the process with the rest of the risotto and cheese. Place the croquettes in the refrigerator to chill for 30 minutes.

5. When you are ready to fry the croquettes, pour oil to a depth of 3 inches in a stockpot or Dutch oven, place it over medium-high heat, and heat it to 375°F. Place a wire rack on a baking sheet and set it near the stove.

6. When the oil reaches 375°F, fry the croquettes, four or five at a time, until golden brown all over, about 5 minutes. Maintain the oil temperature between 365° and 375°F. Transfer the croquettes to the wire rack to drain, and continue frying the rest of the croquettes. Serve warm.

CHILES RELLENOS

SERVES 4

Chiles relleños is one of the most popular dishes in Mexican restaurants, both in Mexico and in the States. They can be stuffed with meat, beans, or a good melting cheese such as Monterey Jack or Cheddar. In this updated version, I've added some goat cheese flavored with a little garlic and thyme to the stuffing. I serve them as an appetizer, topped with Grilled Tomato Hot Sauce thinned with a little chicken stock. You can use any of the large fresh green chile peppers, such as poblanos, Anaheims, or New Mexicos, but poblanos are traditional and work best.

Grilled Tomato Hot Sauce (page 172)
1 cup homemade chicken or vegetable
    stock, or canned chicken broth
Salt and freshly ground black pepper,
    to taste
8 whole green poblano peppers,
    with no blemishes
¾ pound Monterey Jack cheese,
    grated (about 3 cups)
¼ pound fresh goat cheese
    (about ½ cup)
1 tablespoon olive oil
1 clove garlic, minced
½ teaspoon fresh thyme leaves
Peanut or olive oil for frying
¼ cup plus 1 tablespoon all-purpose flour
4 large eggs, separated

1. Place the tomato sauce and stock in a small saucepan over low heat to warm through while you prepare the chiles. Season the broth with salt and pepper.

2. Roast the peppers: Using a long-handled fork, hold the peppers over a gas flame until the skin blisters and turns black all over. (Or roast them under your oven broiler, turning them with tongs as the skin chars.) Burn only the skin—not the flesh—of the peppers. Place the peppers in a plastic bag and close it tight; the skin will steam away from the flesh in about 10 minutes. Then hold the peppers gingerly and let a trickle of cold water run over them as you rub the skin off. (You may want to wear rubber gloves because the poblanos can irritate the skin.) Do not tear the flesh of the peppers. Place them on a work surface and cut a slit down the length of each pepper. Use your index finger to gently remove the seeds. (If necessary, use the tip of a small knife, but do not cut the flesh around the stem.) Rinse under trickling water, then pat each pepper dry, both inside and out.

3. Mix the grated Jack and goat cheese together in a bowl. Place the olive oil in a small sauté pan over medium-low heat, and add the garlic; cook it for about 5 minutes but do not let it brown. Add the garlic and oil to the cheese mixture, and mix well; add the thyme as well.

4. Pour oil to a depth of about 1 inch in a skillet, place it over medium heat, and heat it to 375°F. Preheat the oven to 200°F. Place a wire rack on a baking sheet and set it in the oven.

5. Place the ¼ cup flour on a plate. Stuff each pepper with the cheese mixture, then carefully squeeze the pepper back into its original shape, closing the slit so that no cheese shows. Dredge the peppers in the flour, dusting off any excess, and set aside.

6. In a large bowl, beat the egg whites with ¼ teaspoon salt until they hold soft peaks.

Beat the yolks in another bowl, then fold them into the whites along with the remaining 1 tablespoon flour, working gently but thoroughly.

7. When the oil reaches 375°F, hold each pepper by the stem and dredge it again in the flour. Dust off the excess flour, then dip it in the batter. Lay the peppers in the skillet, without crowding them, and fry until golden on each side, 3 to 4 minutes total. Carefully transfer the peppers to the wire rack to drain and stay warm while you fry the remaining peppers.

8. To serve, divide the broth among four pasta bowls, and gently place two of the peppers in each bowl. Serve immediately.

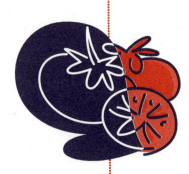

CHAPTER 4

FISH AND SHELLFISH

If this chapter seems to be a long one, it's because there's nothing better—not in my mind, anyway—than fried fish. The first food I remember really falling for was fried bream, a sweet southern sunfish rarely larger than your hand. Mama would lightly dust them in fine cornmeal and deep-fry them until the tails and fins curled up crunchy—a favored treat to this day. Hushpuppies were always served alongside.

Though we lived an hour inland, we spent as much time as possible on the coast. Soon I was proficient at casting shrimp nets and finding the biggest oysters, and while we rarely fried things on the boat, I learned early on the magic of quickly—and barely—cooking those shellfish. To this day I prefer all fish and seafood just barely done. And what better way than to fry it in clean hot fat!

There are basic recipes for fried fish from around the globe in this chapter, as well as some delicious new concoctions from some of today's bright young chefs.

SOUTHERN FRIED FISH AND HUSHPUPPIES

SERVES 8

This is the easiest and most basic of all the fried fish recipes. What makes it southern is the use of corn flour (very finely ground cornmeal) and the addition of hushpuppies. In west Tennessee and throughout the Mississippi River delta, catfish are prepared like this. Throughout the South, other freshwater fish, such as bream (pronounced "brim"), bass, and crappie, are fried with this simple dusting of seasoned corn flour, which produces the crispest crust. Saltwater fish such as whiting are also fried in this manner, but for them wheat flour is usually used. Along the Gulf of Mexico, the fish are likely to be dipped first into an egg wash before coating. But everywhere there's always some cornmeal or corn flour close at hand for hushpuppies. Serve these with Coleslaw or New Potato Salad (see Index).

Peanut oil for frying
1½ cups corn flour, preferably
    stone-ground (see box, facing page)
Salt
½ teaspoon freshly ground
    black pepper
¼ teaspoon cayenne pepper, or
    to taste
1 large egg
2 cups buttermilk
1¾ cups stone-ground whole-grain
    cornmeal (see box, page 41)
½ cup minced onion
1 scant teaspoon baking powder
1 scant teaspoon baking soda
3 pounds small cleaned whole fish
    or fillets, preferably freshwater
    catfish or sunfish

1. Pour oil to a depth of at least 1½ inches in a stockpot or Dutch oven, place it over medium-high heat, and heat it to 375°F. Preheat the oven to 200°F. Place wire racks on two baking sheets, and set them aside.

2. While the oil is heating, prepare the coating for the fish: In a wide bowl, mix the corn flour, 1 teaspoon salt, black pepper, and cayenne.

3. Prepare the hushpuppy batter: Mix the egg and buttermilk well in a medium-size bowl. Then stir in the cornmeal until well blended. Stir in the onion. Measure the baking powder, baking soda, and 1 scant teaspoon salt into a small bowl, and set both bowls aside while you fry the fish.

4. When the oil reaches 375°F, dip each fish or fillet in the seasoned corn flour, coating it all over but shaking off any excess. Carefully lower each piece into the hot oil. Fill the pot but do not crowd it; the oil should bubble up around each piece of fish. Monitor the temperature closely so that it stays between 365° and 375°F. Fry the fish until it is golden all over, turning the pieces, if necessary. It will take 2 to 3 minutes on each side, depending on the size of the pieces. Set aside any of the remaining corn flour.

5. Remove the fish from the oil in the same order that they were immersed, using a wire mesh strainer, tongs, or any tool that will allow you to hold the fish over the pot so excess oil can drain back into the pot. Immediately place the pieces on a wire rack, and place it in the oven to keep them warm.

6. Continue frying until all of the fish are done, always waiting for the oil to return to the proper temperature before adding more fish to the pot. Then proceed with frying the hushpuppies.

7. Add the reserved baking powder mixture to the hushpuppy batter and mix well. Then add the leftover seasoned corn flour to the batter, a little at a time, until the batter is thick enough to be spooned. This will take about ¼ to ½ cup of the remaining corn flour.

8. Make sure that the oil has returned to 375°F, and then drop the batter by spoonfuls into the hot oil, using two teaspoons: one to scoop up the batter and the other to scrape it off and into the oil. Fry the hushpuppies until they are golden brown all over, about 3 minutes, again carefully monitoring the temperature of the oil. Drain each pup well over the pot as it is removed from the oil, and then place them on a wire rack. You probably won't have to put the hushpuppies in the oven to stay warm because your guests will be picking at them. Besides, they stay warm a fairly long time, and there are plenty to go around. Repeat the process until all the batter is fried. Serve the fish and hushpuppies immediately.

CORN FLOUR AND CORNMEAL

Corn flour is the finest grind of cornmeal; in Louisiana it's called "fish fry." If you can't find it, you can make your own by grinding cornmeal in a blender or food processor. I have whole-grain cornmeal and corn flour ground for me in the mountains of Georgia. If you can't find good cornmeal, you can order it from my bookstore, Hoppin' Johns®, in Charleston, (803-577-6404).

FRIED SHARK

SERVES 8

Though shark is caught in coastal waters around the world, it is only fairly recently that Americans have begun to eat it. It is the perfect fish for the fryer because it is devoid of annoying bones. Don't be put off if the shark flesh has an ammonia odor. In shark (unlike other seafood), this is actually a sign of freshness. The smell will disappear when it cooks. Be sure to make hushpuppies to accompany this dish too, following the recipe on the previous page.

3 pounds small shark steaks or cubed shark meat
About 2 cups buttermilk
1 cup corn flour (or 1½ cups if making hushpuppies as well), preferably stone-ground (see box, page 41)
1 teaspoon salt
½ teaspoon freshly ground black pepper
¼ teaspoon cayenne pepper, or to taste
Peanut oil for frying

1. Several hours before you plan to serve the fish, place it in a nonreactive container such as a stainless-steel mixing bowl or a glass baking dish and pour the buttermilk over it, making sure each piece is well covered.

Place the dish in the refrigerator until 1 hour before cooking time.

2. Remove the fish from the refrigerator and place it in a colander to drain and to come to room temperature. Discard the buttermilk.

3. In a wide bowl, mix the corn flour, salt, black pepper, and cayenne. Set aside.

4. Pour oil to a depth of at least 1½ inches in a stockpot or Dutch oven, place it over medium-high heat, and heat it to 375°F.

5. Preheat the oven to its lowest setting. Place a wire rack on a baking sheet, and set it in the oven.

6. If you're making hushpuppies, prepare the batter as described on page 41, and set it aside while you fry the fish.

7. When the oil reaches 375°F, remove the shark from the colander one piece at a time, and coat it in the seasoned corn flour,

shaking off any excess. Carefully lower each piece into the hot oil. Fill the pot, but do not crowd it; the oil should bubble up around each piece of fish. Monitor the temperature closely so that it stays between 365° and 375°F. Fry the fish until it is golden all over, turning the pieces if necessary. It will take 2 to 3 minutes on each side, depending on the size of the pieces. Set aside the remaining corn flour for the hushpuppies if you're making them.

8. Remove the fish from the oil in the same order that the pieces were immersed, using a wire mesh strainer, tongs, or any tool that will allow you to hold the fish over the pot so excess oil can drain off. Immediately place the pieces on the wire rack and keep them warm in the oven. Always wait for the oil to return to 375°F before adding more fish to the pot. Continue frying until all of the shark is fried. Then proceed with frying the hushpuppies. Serve immediately.

FRIED FISH

Every country has its version of fried fish. When properly done, it is one of the best dishes on earth. As Virginia Elverson says in her remarkable cookbook, *Gulf Coast Cooking,* "When it is done well, it is superb. And this depends on three factors: the freshness of the fish (*always* the first factor), the integrity of the coating, and the temperature of the oil or fat." Those coatings are usually the only variables. On the Gulf of Mexico alone, Virginia found cooks coating their fish with seasoned flour, seasoned cornmeal, seasoned chickpea flour, seasoned masa harina, cracker crumbs, flour mixed with nuts or sesame seeds, crushed cornflakes, bread crumbs, cornstarch, and combinations of the above. And then there are the batters!

Here you'll find several recipes for fried fish—deep-fried, pan-fried, and sautéed. There are some fancy restaurant dishes as well as some good ol' down-home food. Everyone seems to have a favorite fried fish dish!

JESSICA'S PORGIES

SERVES 6

This recipe is inspired by one that Jessica Harris, the eminent scholar of the African diaspora, included in her marvelous collection of African-American foods, *The Welcome Table*. If we are to believe the well-known African-American statesman she quotes, cheese grits and fried porgies are *the* definitive African-American dishes.

Porgies are one of my favorite fishes, too. Their firm, sweet flesh takes well to the fryer. If you can't find southern porgies, you can substitute scup or sea bream in this recipe. Serve them, as Jessica recommends, with Basic Hot Pepper Sauce and Coleslaw (see Index).

1 tablespoon crab boil, such as Old Bay
½ cup fresh lemon juice
12 whole porgies or scups, about
½ to ¾ pound each, scaled, gutted,
and heads removed
Peanut oil for frying
⅓ cup mayonnaise
½ cup corn flour (see box, page 41)
Salt and freshly ground black pepper,
to taste

1. Grind the crab boil in a spice mill or blender until it is powdery, and then mix it with the lemon juice.

2. Place the fish in a large shallow bowl, and pour the lemon juice mixture over them. Allow them to sit for about 1 hour.

3. Pour oil to a depth of about 2 inches in a wide heavy pan, place it over medium heat, and heat it to 365°F. Preheat the oven to 200°F. Place a wire rack on a baking sheet and put it in the oven.

4. While the oil is heating, remove the fish from the marinade and rinse them briefly under cold running water. Slather the fish on both sides with the mayonnaise.

5. Scoop the corn flour into a paper bag, and add salt and pepper. Place the fish in the bag, one or two at a time, and shake the bag so that they are well covered with the corn flour.

6. When the oil reaches 365°F, fry the fish for 2 or 3 minutes on each side, or until they are golden brown. Place the fish on the wire rack to drain and stay warm in the oven while you finish cooking all the fish. Serve them immediately.

FISH AND CHIPS

SERVES 4

This is the English version of deep-fried fish and French fries. Anyone who thinks you can't get good food in England hasn't been to a good fish-and-chips shop and had delicious batter-fried haddock or cod served wrapped in newspaper and doused with malt vinegar and salt. Nothing could be better with a pint of ale! The traditional medium for frying fish and chips in England is melted beef fat, but many fry shops have switched to vegetable oils. I use lard or peanut oil. Some of the batters call for flour, baking powder, and water; others include milk and egg. In this one, a little beer is added.

Though I love to fry fish for a crowd, I limit this meal to four people so I'm not at the fryer all evening. For the lightest possible batter, allow it to sit at room temperature for about an hour before you begin; it also helps to use flat, room-temperature beer. If you're using a dark stout, add water to the batter; with a pale ale or lager, add milk.

1 cup all-purpose flour
1 teaspoon salt
1 large egg, separated
¼ cup beer, preferably flat and
    at room temperature
¼ cup milk or water (see headnote)
2 pounds russet (Idaho) potatoes
Peanut oil or lard for deep-frying
2 pounds skinless fish fillets of
    haddock, cod, flounder, or sole,
    ⅜ inch thick and 5 inches long
Malt vinegar, for serving
Salt, for serving

1. About 1 hour before you plan to fry the fish, make the batter: Mix the flour and salt in a mixing bowl. In another bowl, stir together the egg yolk, beer, and milk. Then pour this into the dry ingredients, stirring (but not beating) the mixture well with a wire whisk. Set the batter aside at room temperature to rest.

2. After about 45 minutes, cut the potatoes into ⅜-inch sticks 3 or more inches long and place them in a bowl. Cover them with cold water, and stir them a bit to help remove the excess starch.

3. Pour oil to a depth of 3 or 4 inches in a stockpot or Dutch oven, place it over medium-high heat, and heat it to 375°F. Preheat the oven to 200°F. Place a wire rack on a baking sheet and set it in the oven.

4. Drain the potatoes well, rinse them under running water, and lay them out on a terry-cloth towel, patting them completely dry. When the oil reaches 375°F, fry the potatoes, in batches, until they are thoroughly browned, 8 to 10 minutes. Do not crowd the pot, and carefully maintain the temperature at 375°F. As they are finished, transfer the potatoes to the wire rack to drain and stay warm.

5. While the last batch of potatoes is frying, beat the egg white to soft peaks and gently but thoroughly fold it into the batter. Rinse the fish fillets and pat them dry. Using tongs, drop several pieces of fish at a time into the batter, and then transfer them to the hot oil to fry. Each batch will take about 4 minutes. Remember to maintain the heat at 375°F. Serve hot, and pass the malt vinegar and salt.

FRIED FLOUNDER

SERVES 2

This is one of my favorite dishes. It is the classic French preparation *à la meunière,* or pan-fried in butter. It is most easily prepared one fish at a time in a pan shaped roughly like the fish itself, so I recommend this as a meal for two. Fry yours first, put it on a warmed plate in a low oven, then fry your companion's. Serve it with Pan-Fried Potatoes (see Index) and a green vegetable.

**2 whole flounders, ¾ pound each,
    cleaned (with or without the head)
Salt and freshly ground black pepper
¼ cup all-purpose flour
6 tablespoons (¾ stick) unsalted butter
1 lemon, halved**

1. Preheat the oven to the lowest setting, and place two dinner plates in it to warm.

2. Season the fish with salt and pepper to taste, and then dredge it in the flour, dusting off any excess.

3. Melt 3 tablespoons of the butter in an oblong or 10-inch round skillet over medium-high heat. When the butter has melted and stopped sputtering and hissing, add one of the fish to the pan, white side down. Fry until golden brown, about 3 minutes, and then fry the other side. Transfer the fish to one of the warmed plates, squeeze lemon juice all over it and then pour the browned butter over it. Keep the fish warm while you quickly wipe out the pan and repeat with the second fish. Serve immediately.

SESAME FRIED FISH

SERVES 4

I developed this recipe when I was working on my book of new southern foods. Sesame seeds were brought to the South from West Africa with the slave trade and have remained firmly entrenched in the region's cooking. Use black sea bass, sea bream, porgy, or small snappers for this delicious cross-cultural dish. Small whole fish (gutted) or fillets with the skin on both work well. Serve this with hot sauce and with the green vegetable of your choice.

1½ to 2 pounds fish fillets, or 4 small
  whole fish, cleaned, each less than
  1 pound
Salt and freshly ground black pepper,
  to taste
¼ cup all-purpose flour
¼ cup sesame seeds
2 large eggs
1 tablespoon sesame oil or chile
  sesame oil
¼ to ½ cup peanut oil
Hot sauce, preferably homemade
  (page 175) or your choice

1. Pat the fish dry and season them with salt and pepper. Spread the flour out on a piece of wax paper. Place each fillet or whole fish in the flour and coat both sides well. Dust off any excess. Add the sesame seeds to the remaining flour and mix well.

2. Set out a large plate or a platter.

3. In a large shallow container, beat the eggs with the sesame oil. Dip each fish or fillet in the egg mixture, then in the flour-sesame mix, coating it well, and then place it on the platter. When all of the fish are coated, place the platter in the refrigerator for about 10 minutes.

4. Preheat the oven to 200°F. Place a wire rack on a baking sheet and set it in the oven. Place four dinner plates in the oven to warm.

5. Pour the peanut oil into a large heavy skillet or sauté pan to a depth of ½ inch. Heat the oil over medium-high heat until it is very hot but not smoking. Just as the surface begins to ripple, take the fish out of the refrigerator and place as many in the pan as will fit without crowding, flesh side down.

6. Fry the fish until they are golden brown, about 3 minutes on each side. Transfer the cooked pieces to the wire rack to stay warm while you finish cooking the rest. Divide the fish among the warmed plates, and splash them with hot sauce. Serve immediately.

WHOLE FRIED FISH WITH SPICY THAI SAUCE

SERVES 6

Throughout Asia and in Asian restaurants everywhere, whole fish are fried in woks, doused with a sweet-and-sour sauce, and served to the delight of diners. You can fry any firm-fleshed whole round fish, such as snapper or sea bass, like this as long as you have a pan big enough to hold the entire fish. A large wok will accommodate a two-pound fish. I have a cast-iron pan that is twelve inches wide and twenty inches long; it fits over two burners. I can fry an even larger fish in it.

A two-pound fish will feed six people. If you don't have a big enough pan, use smaller fish and adjust the frying times accordingly. Thai cooking expert Nancie McDermott recommends an electric wok for this technique, because you can plug it in away from the stove, where it will be firmly balanced.

In China, whole fried fish are often served with a sauce made of fermented black beans or hot chiles. I prefer this sauce, made with tamarind. Though uncommon in the United States, the pods of this tropical tree are a staple ingredient in Southeast Asia, India, the Middle East, Africa, and Latin America. You can find it in ethnic markets and the Asian sec-

tion of some supermarkets. It comes in rectangular blocks of pulp (storable indefinitely at room temperature), tastes like citrusy prunes, and has a sweet-and-sour character all its own.

The sauce for this fish also contains red curry paste, which is available in Thai markets and many supermarkets. If you can't find the ingredients to make this Thai dish, go ahead and fry an entire fish, drizzle it with any of the Asian dipping sauces (see Index), and garnish it with plenty of slivered scallions and cilantro. This recipe is adapted from Nancie's book, *Real Thai.*

½ cup hot water

¼ cup tamarind pulp (see
  headnote)

½ cup (or more) vegetable oil
  for frying

1 cup cornstarch or all-purpose flour

1 whole firm-fleshed fish, such as red
  snapper, cod, or sea bass (1½ to 2
  pounds), scaled and gutted but
  with the head intact

4 large cloves garlic, minced

1 tablespoon red curry paste
  (see headnote)

6 tablespoons Asian fish sauce,
  such as *nam pla* (see Note, page 184)

¼ cup soy sauce

¼ cup (loosely packed) light or
  dark brown sugar

3 scallions, thinly sliced

1 tablespoon minced fresh ginger

Cilantro leaves, cucumber slices,
  and halved cherry tomatoes,
  for garnish

1. Pour the hot water over the tamarind pulp and allow it to sit for 20 minutes, until it is cool enough to handle. Using your fingertips, work the pulp free of the seeds. Then strain the liquid through a fine-mesh sieve, pushing as much pulp through as possible. Set it aside.

2. Pour the oil into a wok or a heavy pan that is larger than the fish (pans other than woks may need more oil). Place the wok over medium-high heat, and heat the oil to 375°F. Place a wire rack on a baking sheet and set aside.

3. While the oil is heating, spread the cornstarch out on a sheet of wax paper that is longer than the fish. Rinse the fish and pat it completely dry, inside and out. Cut several diagonal gashes in the thickest part of the flesh, down to the bone. Place the fish in the cornstarch, and lift each side of the wax paper to cradle the fish and dust it well. Turn it over and dust the other side well; then shake off the excess.

4. When the oil reaches 375°F, carefully lower the fish into the wok, using two spatulas. Immediately raise the heat a little, and fry the fish until the first side is golden, about 5 minutes, diligently maintaining the oil temperature between 365° and 375°F. Carefully turn the fish over, using the spatulas, and cook until the second side is browned, about 4 minutes. Remove the fish from the pan and make sure that it is cooked through by checking the flesh at one of the gashes. It should be opaque. Place the fish on the wire rack to drain.

5. Lower the heat to medium, and pour off all but 2 tablespoons of the oil. Add the garlic and count to ten, stir-frying so that the garlic doesn't brown. Add the curry paste, breaking it all up and distributing it in the pan. After 1 minute, add ½ cup of the reserved tamarind liquid, the fish sauce, the soy sauce, and the brown sugar. Cook until the sugar has dissolved and the sauce has thickened, about 1 minute more. Stir in the scallions and ginger, reduce the heat, and simmer for 2 minutes more. During this last simmer, transfer the fish to a serving platter.

6. The sauce should be shiny and thick. Pour it over the fish and garnish with the cilantro, cucumbers, and tomato halves. Serve immediately.

PICKLED FRIED FISH

SERVES 8

Escabèche, fried fish that is pickled and served cold, appears on plates everywhere the Spanish and Portuguese settled. A virtually identical dish is found in Malaysia and in South Africa. Being great slave and spice traders, the Iberians long had relations with Malaysia. I wonder who taught whom the recipe! It remains popular today in the Mediterranean, the Azores, and Cuba.

Though any fish can be prepared like this, I recommend using a strong-flavored one that won't fall apart. Oily kingfish and salmon work well, as does swordfish. The whole preparation is done a day ahead. Serve as an appetizer.

½ cup olive oil

2 pounds firm fish, cut into eight
    1-inch-thick pieces or 1½-inch cubes

½ cup all-purpose flour

2 medium onions, thinly sliced

2 cloves garlic, minced

¾ cup distilled white vinegar

1 tablespoon chopped fresh parsley

1 bay leaf, crumbled

Salt and freshly ground black pepper,
    to taste

1 green bell pepper, cored, seeded,
    and cut into rings

1 jalapeño pepper, seeded, deribbed,
    and minced (optional)

1. The day before you plan to serve the fish, line a colander with crumpled paper towels.

2. Pour ¼ cup of the oil into a large heavy skillet, and heat it over medium heat until it is hot but not smoking.

3. Dust the fish with the flour, and fry until it is golden on all sides, 5 to 10 minutes. Place the fish in the colander to drain and cool to room temperature.

4. When all the fish is fried, wipe out the pan and add the remaining ¼ cup oil. Sauté the onions and garlic until limp, about 5 minutes. Then add the vinegar, parsley, bay leaf, salt, and pepper. Bring to a boil, reduce the heat, and simmer for 10 minutes. Allow the marinade to cool.

5. Place the cooled fish in a shallow glass baking dish, add the bell pepper and the jalapeño, and pour the cooled marinade over the fish. Cover and marinate in the refrigerator for 24 hours before draining and serving.

FISH WITH A POTATO CRUST

SERVES 4

This recipe is an adaptation of one from Jamie Shannon, the chef at the venerable Commander's Palace in New Orleans. He serves his with a lemon butter sauce, but I like to serve it in summer with a quickly made sauce of fresh tomatoes and sweet local onions. Though actually a variation of a French dish popularized by the Lyonnais chef Paul Bocuse, this is also a modern version of fish and chips (with ketchup).

Assemble all of the ingredients before beginning this recipe. Make the Tomato Sauce first, and then proceed with the fish recipe.

4 baking potatoes, about ¾ pound each
1 large egg
½ cup milk
Salt and freshly ground black pepper
1 cup all-purpose flour
4 trout (or other firm white-fleshed fish) fillets, about ¼ pound each
½ cup olive oil
Tomato Sauce (page 170), heated
1 lemon, quartered, for serving

1. Peel the potatoes and cut them into thin shoestrings or julienne strips, using a mandoline if you have one. Spread half of the potatoes out on a damp kitchen towel, covering an area just big enough to accommodate the trout fillets in a single layer.

2. Using a whisk, beat the egg with the milk in a wide bowl. Mix 1 teaspoon salt and ½ tea-spoon pepper with the flour in another wide bowl. Season the fillets on both sides with salt and pepper.

3. Dredge the fillets in the flour, shaking off any excess. Dip the fillets in the egg mixture, and then place them on top of the potatoes. Cover the fish with the remaining potatoes. Cover with another kitchen towel (it's not necessary to dampen it), and lightly but firmly press so the potatoes will stick on both sides of the fillets.

4. Preheat the oven to its lowest setting, and place a wire rack on a baking sheet in the oven.

5. Heat the oil in a large skillet or sauté pan over medium-high heat, letting it approach the smoking point. Just as the surface begins to ripple, uncover the fish, and using a wide metal spatula, carefully lift two of the potato-

encrusted fillets, placing them in the hot oil. Do not disturb the fish for several minutes. You want the potatoes to form a golden crust, which will release itself from the bottom of the pan when the sugars in the potatoes caramelize. Turn down the heat if the potatoes appear to be cooking too rapidly—they should take about 6 minutes on each side.

6. After about 5 minutes on this first side, peek under the fish to see if the potatoes are fully browned. They should have loosened from the bottom of the pan. Use a knife or a sharp metal spatula to slice the two potato-encrusted fillets apart. Then carefully turn each to cook on the other side, using two

spatulas if necessary. Carefully remove the cooked fillets from the pan, being sure to let any excess oil drain back into the pan. Place the fillets on the rack in the oven.

7. Turn the oven off, and place four dinner plates in it to warm.

8. Remove any bits of potato from the oil while it is reheating. Then continue with the second batch of fish. When they are cooked, place the fish on the rack in the oven to drain. Remove the plates from the oven, and spoon a pool of the Tomato Sauce onto each plate. Arrange the potato-encrusted fish on top of the sauce, and serve with the lemon quarters.

ABOUT SALT COD

Fried cakes of salt cod are found throughout the Mediterranean and Caribbean, even though the fish is from the North Atlantic. Though modern refrigeration long ago replaced the need for drying and salting, the food is so firmly entrenched in the cooking of some regions that the natives, it is said, actually prefer "stockfish" (dried cod) and *baccalà* (Italian for salt cod) to fresh fish.

Slaves in the Caribbean were fed inexpensive salt cod from New England. Throughout the Greater and Lesser Antilles, descendants of both master and slave prepare a world of dishes with salt

cod today. It's still popular in New England as well. "Stamp and go" is Jamaica's salt cod fritter; in the Azores they're called "dreams"—*sonhos de bacalhau*. Even in France's great wine region, Bordeaux, with its world of fresh fish, salt cod often finds its way to the table.

If you've never tried it, go to an Italian, West Indian, or Hispanic market and buy some. You'll be surprised how delicious it can be. Simply soak ¾ pound of salt cod overnight in several changes of water. Flake the fish, and use it in place of salmon in the croquette recipe on the following page, omitting the salt.

SALMON CROQUETTES

SERVES 6

Croquettes like these can be made with all sorts of cooked fish and meats, but salmon is traditional. I've made them with canned salmon and served them to food critics and they've loved them; you can also use salt cod (see box on opposite page). Dill is the herb to use with salmon; parsley works better with more delicately flavored fish.

1 pound flaked cooked salmon or
　　other fish, or 1 can (14¾ ounces)
　　salmon, drained and flaked
2 tablespoons minced onion
1 pound (about 2 average) Idaho
　　potatoes, cooked, peeled, and
　　mashed
2 large eggs, beaten
3 tablespoons chopped fresh dill,
　　parsley, or other herb of your choice
2 tablespoons peanut oil or clarified
　　butter (page 8)
¼ cup cornmeal
Salt and freshly ground black pepper,
　　to taste
2 lemons, quartered, or Tartar Sauce
　　(page 164), for serving

1. Combine the fish, onion, mashed potatoes, eggs, and herbs in a large bowl and mix well. Divide the mixture into twelve patties.

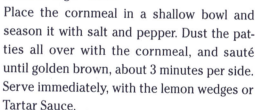

2. Put the oil in a large well-seasoned skillet, and place it over medium-high heat. Place the cornmeal in a shallow bowl and season it with salt and pepper. Dust the patties all over with the cornmeal, and sauté until golden brown, about 3 minutes per side. Serve immediately, with the lemon wedges or Tartar Sauce.

PAN-FRIED TROUT WITH BACON

SERVES 2

This is classic campfire cooking, found wherever freshwater anglers catch trout. All you need is some good bacon, a little cornmeal or flour for dusting the fish, a frying pan, and the trout. If you were in the wild, you would welcome some onions and potatoes added to the pan and warmed through, but at home some may not appreciate the fishy-flavored vegetables. At any rate, you'll probably want to serve a simple starch with the meal. A lemon is all the seasoning you'll need with the fish. You won't even need salt and pepper if your bacon is the good country-style kind.

I've given instructions for cooking whole fish, but you can use gutted and split fish or fillets as well. Just don't overcook it. All fish is done when it just barely flakes from the bone; any more cooking and it loses both texture and flavor. This recipe serves two, but you can multiply it without fear. If you are planning to cook this on a fishing expedition, take the meal or flour in a large, heavy self-seal plastic bag. You can dust the fish right in it.

4 slices bacon
½ cup corn flour (see box, page 41),
    or ¼ cup cornmeal plus ¼ cup
    all-purpose flour
2 fresh mountain trout, about ¾ pound
    each, gutted but heads intact
1 lemon, halved, for serving
1 small onion, sliced (optional)
2 to 3 medium potatoes, cooked and
    quartered (optional)

1. Place a large heavy skillet over medium heat and cook the bacon in it until it is crisp and completely rendered of fat. Set the bacon aside to drain on paper towels while you fry the fish.

2. Place the corn flour in a large self-seal plastic bag. Cut two small gashes in the thickest part of each side of the fish. Put the fish, one at a time, into the plastic bag and shake to coat with the corn flour. Place the fish immediately in the hot bacon grease, and cook until browned on both sides, about 10 to 12 minutes in all. Serve immediately, with the lemon halves and bacon. If you like, increase the heat to medium-high and toss the onion and potatoes in the pan to warm them through, and serve with the trout.

SAGE AND ANCHOVY MICE

MAKES ABOUT 20 TIDBITS

These little deep-fried tidbits of anchovies sandwiched between fresh sage leaves are disarmingly delightful, looking as they do, with their tails, like mice. Serve them with aperitifs. They are adapted from a recipe in Johanne Killeen and George Germon's cookbook *Cucina Simpatica,* which features the delicious food served in their Providence, Rhode Island, trattoria, Al Forno.

If you have a sage plant in your herb garden, you may find, as I do, that it gets enormous between uses. It will benefit from the trimming that this recipe requires.

Peanut oil for deep-frying
1 tin (2 ounces) good-quality flat
  anchovy fillets
½ cup all-purpose flour
1 large egg
36 to 48 large fresh sage leaves
  with stems

1. Pour oil to a depth of 3 or 4 inches in a stockpot or Dutch oven, place it over medium heat, and heat it to 380°F. Place a wire rack on a baking sheet and set it aside.

2. While the oil is heating, drain the anchovies in a sieve, and rinse them under lukewarm water. Lay them out flat on paper towels and blot them dry. You should have 9 to 12 fillets. Cut each in half.

3. Put the flour in a shallow bowl. Place several paper towels and a small plate on your work surface. Lightly beat the egg in a shallow bowl with a rim, such as a soup plate or pasta bowl. Holding a sage leaf by its stem, drag it through the egg and lay it on the plate, upside down. Place one of the anchovy pieces on it. Then drag another sage leaf through the egg and place it on top of the anchovy, right side up. Holding the "sandwich" by the stems, drag it again through the egg, then through the flour. Place it on a paper towel while you repeat the process with all the sage leaves and anchovies.

4. When the oil reaches 380°F, begin placing the little "mice" in the hot oil, carefully lowering them by their "tails." A large stockpot should hold all of them without crowding. Cook for 1 minute on each side, removing them in the order in which they were added to the pot. Place them on the wire rack to drain. Serve immediately.

SHAD ROE AND BACON

SERVES 1 (CAN BE EASILY MULTIPLIED)

Shad are anadromous fish like salmon and herring; they live in the open sea but spawn in rivers. They appear as soon as the river water warms: as early as January in northern Florida's St. Johns River, as late as May in upper New England, when they also appear on the West Coast. The flesh takes well to frying, but it is full of bones. The bright red roe, however, is succulent and intensely flavored. It is traditionally fried with bacon. Two methods follow, one for deep-frying and another for pan-frying.

Each female shad carries two sacs of roe. They can weigh from just a couple of ounces to over half a pound. If they are small, you may want to serve two to each diner as an entrée, or one as an appetizer. The roe is rich. I try to buy medium sets (of two sacs), weighing about twelve ounces, and serve one sac per person. The deep-fried roe can also be cut up for an hors d'oeuvre. I like to serve the pan-fried version with grits.

FOR DEEP-FRYING
1 medium shad roe sac per person
1 or 2 slices of bacon per person
Oil for deep-frying
Lemon wedges, for serving

1. Wrap each sac in bacon and secure it with toothpicks. Place the roe on a wax-paper-lined pan and freeze it for about 10 minutes.

2. Pour oil to a depth of 3 inches in a stockpot or Dutch oven, and place it over medium-high heat. When it reaches 365°F, fry the roe until the bacon is crisp and the roe is golden, about 6 minutes. Serve immediately, with lemon wedges.

FOR PAN-FRYING
1 medium shad roe sac per person
2 slices of bacon per person
Lemon wedges, for serving

1. Place the roe in a skillet, cover with water, and simmer for 2 minutes or so to firm it. Drain on paper towels. Pat dry.

2. Fry the bacon in a heavy skillet over medium heat until crisp and completely rendered of fat, about 10 minutes. Set the bacon aside to drain on paper towels.

3. Place the roe in the hot bacon grease, flat side down. Cook until golden brown, about 4 minutes; then turn to brown the other side briefly, about 2 minutes. Serve immediately, with lemon wedges and the bacon.

Garlicky Cottage Cheese Salad

- 16 oz tub cottage cheese
- 2 fresh chopped tomatoes
- 3 green onions, chopped coarsely
- 1 tsp **Garli Garni**
- 1/4 C chopped pickled garlic
- 1 Tbls olive oil
- 1 Tbls **Garlic Festival Wine Vinegar**

Mix the above ingredients in a large bowl. Chill thoroughly, pack in a crock and serve with crackers or baguettes.

Skordalia

A delicious vegetarian appetizer

- 1 lb baking potatoes; cooked soft, cooled, & peeled
- 2 lg fresh garlic cloves, minced fine
- 1 tsp **Garli Garni**
- 1/4-1/2 C virgin olive oil
- 2 Tbls fresh lemon juice

Mash by hand until smooth. Pound garlic & salt to a smooth paste & add to the potatoes. Beating steadily, add oil slowly to make a smooth mixture Stir in lemon juice. Serve warm or cool with pita wedges or crackers.

Garli Garni Pull Apart Bread

- 1 pkg. frozen bread dough
- 4 Tbls butter or margarine
- **Garli Garni** to taste
- your choice fresh herbs

Thaw dough per instructions. Melt butter & sprinkle in Garli Garni & chopped herbs. Separate dough into 2"round pieces & roll in **Garli Garni**/herb butter to coat. Arrange in deep baking dish. Top with remaining butter and bake according to package instructions. This also works great with **Garli Ghetti!**

An all time favorite!

Lo Cal Linguine & Clams

You'll never miss the oil or butter. Pour canned clams with juice into skillet. Sprinkle in **Garli Garni** to taste. Sprinkle in a packet of Butter Buds (diet food section) or Molly McButter. Mix & simmer uncovered until liquid reduces by about 1/3. Meanwhile, cook pasta to al dente and drain. Toss with clam sauce & top with fresh grated Parmesan cheese & chopped parsley.

Pasta Pronto

• Serve your choice of cooked pasta tossed with **GF Stir Fry Sauce** for a spicy treat. • or try pasta with cream, **Garli Ghetti** & cooked baby shrimp (or mushrooms, artichoke hearts, sun dried tomatoes, diced cooked poultry etc.) • BE CREATIVE! Try pasta tossed with **GF Salsa** or • toss **pasta with GF Mop Sauce or Italian Scallion Dressing** and chopped vegetables & cooked chicken or tuna, chilled, for a tangy pasta salad.

Lemon Garli Garni

Use on sauteed or grilled fish, steamed clams or mussels and grilled or roasted poultry.

❄ RECITES ❄

Garlic Festival® Foods

Garli Garni™ Butter

Melt butter in a skillet. Sprinkle in a desired amount of **Garli Garni**. Use on pasta, potatoes, corn on the cob, broccoli, mushrooms, meat, seafood, poultry, bread, soups, sauces, & dressings...

Use your imagination !!

Garlic Rosemary Chicken

- 1 chicken (cut up)
- Garlic Festival Stir Fry Sauce
- **Garli Garni**
- 1 beer • 1 stick butter
- several sprigs (10 or 12) fresh rosemary • • •

Marinate chicken in 1 cup GF Stir Fry overnight in refrigerator. Heat beer in saucepan with butter. Stir in at least 2 Tbls Garli Garni. Tie rosemary onto handle of wooden spoon to make a basting brush. Grill over coals until crispy & done; basting often with beer mixture using rosemary brush

Savory Garlic Smashed Potatoes

- 1/2 C any flavor **pickled garlic** with juice
- 2 lbs new potatoes (cleaned & halved)
- enough chicken or vegetable stock to cover potatoes
- salt & pepper to taste

Place all ingredients except salt & pepper in a microwavable bowl with stock covering potatoes. Micro-wave on high until potatoes are soft. Remove and mash with potato masher to desired consistency. For buttery flavor add Molly McButter (or butter if you don't mind the calories).

Captain's & Mrs. Garlic's Keilbasa Roll Up

- 1 pkg keilbasa sausage
- 1 thawed frozen pizza dough
- 1 egg
- **Garlic Festival® Mustard** (your choice)

Roll out pizza dough & spread with mustard. Place Kielbasa on it & roll up. Pinch ends tightly. Baste the outside with beaten egg & bake in oven according to dough directions. Bake until done & golden brown. Cut into large portions for a meal or small slices for hors d'oeuvres.

Basic Mustard Sauce

Mix **Garlic Festival® Mustard** with an equal amount of sour cream & a grind of fresh black pepper. Stir and heat briefly. For an added touch, stir in a dash of cognac or brandy. Delicious with roast beef, prime rib, steak, ham or sausage.

JIMMY'S SOFT-SHELLS

SERVES 6

I dare say no one in this country knows soft-shells like chef Jimmy Sneed of Richmond. The man is an absolute fanatic about them—even keeps his own tanks so that he can monitor the shedding process and pull the "busters," the ones that are just getting ready to shed, at their tenderest moment.

This recipe of Jimmy's is the classic buttery preparation, a favorite from New Orleans to Baltimore. It is simple and perfectly delicious. Serve these crabs as the main course.

12 live soft-shell crabs
½ cup all-purpose flour
1 cup (2 sticks) unsalted butter,
    clarified (page 8)
3 tablespoons fresh lemon juice
Chopped fresh parsley, for garnish

1. Prepare the crabs for cooking: Turn each crab over on its back, and using sharp scissors, remove the apron by cutting along the edge of the shell where the apron is attached, hingelike, to the body. (The apron contains the reproductive organs. Jimmy says, "A male's apron looks like the Washington Monument; a female's, the Capitol building.") Turn the crab over, and with the scissors at an angle, cut off the eyes and most of the mouth with one cut. Pull out the clear sac behind the eyes and discard it. Lift up the shoulder flaps and cut off the gills. Pat the crab dry.

2. Preheat the oven to 200°F. Place six dinner plates in the oven to warm.

3. Place the flour in a large bowl and dredge the crabs in it one at a time, dusting off any excess. Heat the clarified butter and the lemon juice in a large skillet or sauté pan over medium-high heat. Lay the crabs, face down, in the hot butter (don't crowd the pan). Cook for 1 to 2 minutes, until golden brown. ("Be very careful," Jimmy cautions. "They pop!") Turn the crabs and cook for a minute more on the second side, until browned. Place the crabs on the warmed plates and brush the tops with some of the lemon butter, then sprinkle with parsley. Return them to the oven to keep warm while you fry the rest of the crabs. Serve hot.

TEMPURA SOFT-SHELLS

SERVES 4 AS AN APPETIZER

Soft-shells take well to deep-frying. This light tempura batter includes no egg; it's another one of chef Jimmy Sneed's recipes. You can simply sprinkle the fried crabs with salt and pepper or offer an Asian dipping sauce (see Index).

4 live soft-shell crabs
Peanut or canola oil for deep-frying
2 cups all-purpose flour
1 teaspoon baking soda
1 cup cold water
1 handful ice cubes
Sea salt and freshly ground black
     pepper, to taste

1. Clean the crabs as described in step 1 on page 57. Trim off and discard the legs. Cut the crab down the middle into two pieces, with a claw on each half. Pat the crabs dry.

2. Pour oil to a depth of at least 3 inches in a stock pot or Dutch oven; do not fill the pot more than half full. Heat the oil to 375°F over medium-high heat.

3. While the oil is heating, mix the flour and baking soda in a bowl; then whisk in the cold water. Beat the mixture until it is free of lumps. Add the ice cubes and let it sit for 1 minute. Dredge the crabs in the batter, shaking off any excess batter and ice.

4. When the oil reaches 375°F, fry the crabs until golden brown, just a minute or so; be careful not to let any of the ice cubes fall in the hot oil. Drain on paper towels. Season with salt and pepper, and serve immediately.

SOFT-SHELLS

When soft-shells appear in the market (from late winter through the spring), I try to eat them as often as possible.

The Atlantic blue crab is one of the most delicious creatures alive. It sheds its hard shell a score of times in its three-year life span, and it's just after this shedding that you can eat the whole crab, shell and all. Most preparations for soft-shells are relatively simple—pan-fried in butter, tempura-fried in oil, or simply placed on a hot grill. They can be brushed with mustard and fried like the oysters on page 63 as well; and they're delicious in a Po' Boy with tartar sauce.

SOFT-SHELL CRAB CHORON

SERVES 8

The next time you think that everyone is eating light, take a trip to New Orleans for some hearty Creole fare. Chef Jamie Shannon at the Commander's Palace is known for his elaborate preparations that are true to that city's Creole traditions. This recipe, adapted from one at Commander's, takes time and requires a number of pots, but there's no difficult technique to master. In it, soft-shells are stuffed with crabmeat imperial and raw shrimp, then battered, deep-fried, and topped with tomato-ey Sauce Choron. Bring on the Big Easy (and the easy chair)! You can save time by making the Sauce Choron and the mayonnaise in advance.

Given the enormous popularity of Cajun and Creole foods today, you should have no trouble finding a Creole seasoning mix; look for one that lists paprika as a major ingredient. You can also use a commercial crab boil such as Zatarain's or Old Bay, or an herbal mix, such as herbes de Provence or Italian seasoning, spiked with cayenne; just grind them first.

FOR THE CRABMEAT IMPERIAL
½ cup Blender Mayonnaise (page 162)
¾ pound lump crabmeat, picked over to remove cartilage
¼ cup finely chopped green bell pepper
2 tablespoons finely chopped jarred pimiento or roasted red bell pepper
1 scallion (including a little of the green top), finely chopped
1 teaspoon Worcestershire sauce
Dash of Tabasco sauce
2 teaspoons Dijon mustard
Salt and freshly ground white pepper, to taste

FOR THE CRABS
8 large live soft-shell crabs
16 medium shrimp, shelled and deveined
Peanut oil for deep-frying
1 cup all-purpose flour
1 large egg
1 cup milk
3 teaspoons Creole seasoning mix (see headnote)
2 cups fine dry bread crumbs
Sauce Choron (page 168)

1. Prepare the Crabmeat Imperial: Combine all the ingredients in a bowl, gently mixing them together so as not to break up the crabmeat.

2. Prepare the crabs: Cut the apron off each crab (page 57, step 1); do not remove the face. Lift each shoulder flap and remove the gills. Place a shrimp in each pocket where the gills had been. Carefully remove the soft top of each crab and fill the cavity with the stuffing. Pat the top back into place.

3. Pour oil to a depth of at least 3 inches in a stockpot or Dutch oven. Place it over medium-high heat, and heat it to 365°F. Preheat the oven to 200°F. Place a wire rack on a baking sheet and set it in the oven.

4. While the oil is heating, place the flour in a shallow container, such as a baking dish. In another shallow bowl using a whisk, beat the egg with the milk. Sprinkle 2 teaspoons of the Creole seasoning all over the crabs. In a third shallow bowl, mix the remaining 1 teaspoon Creole seasoning with the bread crumbs.

5. When the oil reaches 365°F, dust each crab with the flour. Dip a pair of tongs in the oil, and then pick up a crab with the tongs and dip it first in the egg mixture, then in the seasoned crumbs. Holding the crab body with the tongs, gently lower the legs—only—into the oil for about 30 seconds, until the legs fold up to the body. Turn the crab over and drop it into the oil, frying it until it is golden brown, about 3 minutes. Repeat the process with the other crabs, but do not crowd the pot. Keep the oil between 350° and 365°F. As each crab is cooked, transfer it to the wire rack in the oven.

6. When all the crabs are done, pat off any excess oil with paper towels and serve them immediately, with the Sauce Choron.

PAN-FRIED CRAB CAKES

SERVES 3 AS A MAIN COURSE OR 6 AS AN APPETIZER

Crab cakes are another of those widely varied regional specialties. In these pan-fried ones, there is neither bread nor mayonnaise; a little mustard and a beaten egg white holds them together. Crab cakes take to a world of accompaniments, from traditional tartar and hollandaise sauces to spicy salsas and coleslaws. I prefer to serve these buttery ones on a pool of Tomato Sauce or Roasted Pepper Purée, or with Chunky Fruit Salsa (see Index), but you can use just about any of the other accompaniments in the Go-Withs chapter.

1 tablespoon fresh lemon juice
1 pound fresh lump crabmeat, picked
    over to remove cartilage
1 tablespoon coarse-grain mustard
2 large eggs, separated
8 tablespoons (1 stick) unsalted butter
2 tablespoons finely chopped onion
½ cup chopped red bell pepper, or
    ¼ cup chopped green bell pepper
1 tablespoon sherry vinegar
1 tablespoon finely chopped fresh herbs
    of your choice
Salt and freshly ground black pepper,
    to taste
Cayenne pepper, to taste
2 cups fine dry bread crumbs

1. Sprinkle the lemon juice over the crabmeat in a large bowl. In a separate small bowl, mix the mustard with the egg yolks.

2. Melt 4 tablespoons of the butter in a skillet over medium-low heat. Add the onion and bell pepper, and cook until the onion begins to become transparent, about 10 minutes. Add the vinegar, raise the heat, and reduce until the vinegar has evaporated. Pour the mixture over the crabmeat.

3. Add the mustard mixture and toss all together, being careful not to break up the big lumps of crabmeat. Season with the fresh herbs, salt, black pepper, and cayenne.

4. Place the bread crumbs in another large mixing bowl. Melt the remaining 4 tablespoons butter in a large skillet or sauté pan over medium heat. Beat the egg whites until they are stiff, and gently fold them into the crab mixture.

5. Using your hands, gently press a portion of the crabmeat mixture into a cake about 3 inches wide and 1 inch thick. Form the rest of the mixture into cakes (six in all). Place the cakes, one at a time, in the bread crumbs. Pour crumbs over the top of the cake. Do not mash or press the crumbs into the cake; you only want a dusting of crumbs *on* the cake, not *in* it. When the butter is foamy, gently pick up the first cake and put it in the pan. Continue dusting the cakes and placing them in the pan; they should all fit into the skillet. Cook until browned on the first side, about 3 minutes; then carefully turn each cake and cook 3 minutes on the other side. Handled carefully, they will not split. Serve immediately.

ROBERT'S CRAB CAKES

SERVES 6 AS AN APPETIZER

These Maryland-style crab cakes come from Charleston caterer Robert Barbato, whose menus usually reflect his Italian heritage. They should really be called Deep-Fried Maryland Crab Balls, as Robert explains: "When I visited a Maryland family, there was a local grocery store that had a deep fryer in it. They used to make the crab cakes the size of baseballs and fry them there in the store. People would take them home and reheat them or eat them hot, in the car on the way home, the way I did. I got the recipe from the family cook." Serve these as an appetizer, with Tartar Sauce (see Index).

Canola oil for deep-frying
1 pound lump crabmeat, picked over
    to remove cartilage
2 large eggs, lightly beaten
2 tablespoons Blender Mayonnaise
    (page 162)
Salt and freshly ground black or
    white pepper, to taste
1 tablespoon Worcestershire sauce
1 to 3 teaspoons dry mustard,
    to taste
1 cup fresh or dry bread crumbs

1. Pour oil to a depth of 3 to 4 inches in a stock pot or Dutch oven, place it over medium to medium-high heat, and heat it to 365°F. Place a wire rack on a baking sheet and set it near the stove.

2. While the oil is heating, place the crabmeat in a large bowl, and add all the remaining ingredients except the bread crumbs, mixing as well as possible without breaking up the crabmeat.

3. Pour the bread crumbs over the crabmeat mixture and begin forming the mixture into 2- to 3-inch balls, using as little of the crumbs as possible but enough to help hold them together.

4. Carefully drop the crab balls into the oil, being sure not to crowd the pot. Maintain the temperature between 365° and 375°F. Do not let the temperature go over 375°F. Fry the balls until golden brown—about 1 minute, depending on their size. Carefully remove the balls from the oil and set them on the wire rack to drain. Pat off any excess oil with paper towels, if necessary, and serve.

OYSTER PO' BOY

SERVES 2

Here's a version of the New Orleans classic, made with oysters that have been painted with mustard before frying. The oysters are perfectly delicious by themselves, or served with any number of sauces, but this sandwich garnished with homemade Tartar Sauce makes a wonderful spring lunch for two.

1 loaf of French or Italian bread, about 15 inches long and 3 inches wide, or 2 hoagie rolls
1 pint shucked oysters, drained
¼ cup all-purpose flour
⅓ cup Dijon mustard
¼ cup corn flour (see box, page 41) or all-purpose flour
Vegetable oil for frying
Tartar Sauce (page 164), chilled
Lettuce leaves or shredded lettuce

1. Preheat the oven to 200°F. Place a wire rack on a baking sheet and put it in the oven.

2. Split the bread lengthwise, and scoop out most of the fluffy center. Place the hollowed-out bread in the oven.

3. Pat the oysters dry. Put the all-purpose flour, mustard, and corn flour in separate shallow bowls or plates. Pour oil to a depth of about ½ inch in a deep skillet, sauté pan, or Dutch oven. Place over medium-high heat, and heat the oil to 365°F.

4. Using one hand to handle the food, dredge the oysters in the all-purpose flour, shaking off any extra. Then dip them in the mustard, and use a pastry brush to paint them evenly with a thin layer of mustard. Place the mustard-coated oysters in the corn flour, and dust them all over. As each oyster is coated, set it aside on a sheet of waxed paper.

5. When the oil reaches 365°F, add the oysters, using tongs, and fry until golden brown all over, about 1½ minutes on each side. Do not crowd the skillet; about six to eight oysters can be fried at one time. As they are done, transfer the oysters to the wire rack to keep warm and drain.

6. Remove the bread from the oven and spread both sides thickly with Tartar Sauce. Then line them with lettuce leaves or shredded lettuce.

7. When all the oysters have been fried, add them to the sandwiches and serve immediately.

DILL FRIED OYSTERS

SERVES 6

This recipe is adapted from Virginia Elverson's book *Gulf Coast Cooking,* for which she traveled from Key West to the tip of the Yucatán peninsula in search of the Gulf's best seafood cookery. They are, as Virginia says, a new twist on fried oysters.

2 large eggs
½ cup plus ⅔ cup finely chopped
    dill pickle
½ cup dill pickle juice
2 teaspoons salt
½ teaspoon freshly ground black pepper
2 pints shucked oysters, drained
½ cup sour cream
¾ cup mayonnaise
Peanut oil for frying
¼ teaspoon dried dill
2 cups all-purpose flour

1. In a large mixing bowl, beat the eggs. Add the ½ cup pickle, the pickle juice, salt, and pepper, and mix well. Add the oysters, making sure they're all coated with the mixture, and marinate, covered, in the refrigerator for 1 hour.

2. Prepare the sauce by mixing the remaining ⅔ cup chopped pickle with the sour cream and mayonnaise. Refrigerate, covered, until ready to serve.

3. Remove the oysters from the refrigerator and place them in a colander to drain. Pour oil to a depth of 2 to 3 inches in a saucepan, place it over medium-high heat, and heat it to 365°F. In a shallow bowl, combine the dill and the flour.

4. When the oil reaches 365°F, dredge the oysters, in batches, in the flour mixture and fry in the hot oil until golden brown all over, 3 to 5 minutes. Drain on paper towels and serve with the dill sauce.

SAUTEED OYSTERS OVER GRITS CAKES

SERVES 4 AS AN APPETIZER OR 2 AS A MAIN COURSE

This recipe—oysters with sherried ham over grits cakes—came to me from South Carolina chef Rob Enniss. Before sautéing the oysters, preheat the oven to its lowest setting. Place a wire rack over a baking sheet and set it in the oven, along with four appetizer plates or two dinner plates. Prepare the grits cakes, and then place them on the wire rack to drain and keep warm until ready to prepare the oysters.

Basic Grits Cakes (page 17)
¼ cup all-purpose flour
20 freshly shucked oysters, with their liquor
Salt and freshly ground black pepper, to taste
¼ cup clarified butter (page 8), or a blend of clarified butter and peanut oil
¼ cup julienned cooked country ham
3 shallots, julienned
1 clove garlic, finely minced
2 tablespoons dry sherry
1 tablespoon chopped fresh sage, or 1 teaspoon dried
2 tablespoons unsalted butter, at room temperature

1. Remove the grits cakes from the oven (see headnote), and divide them among the warmed plates.

2. Place the flour in a shallow bowl. Drain the oysters, reserving the liquor. Place them on a paper towel and pat dry. Season the oysters with salt and pepper, and then roll them in the flour.

3. Melt the clarified butter in a skillet over medium-high heat, and sauté the oysters until golden brown, about 2 minutes on each side. Arrange the cooked oysters on and around the grits cakes.

4. Reduce the heat to medium and add the ham, shallots, and garlic to the same skillet. Sauté gently until barely browned, about 3 minutes. Add the sherry and let it bubble, scraping the pan to deglaze it.

5. Add the reserved oyster liquor and the sage, and cook until a film of liquid remains, about 5 minutes. Remove the skillet from the heat and add the butter. Melt it by gently swirling the skillet. Correct the seasoning with salt and pepper, and then pour the sauce over the oysters and grits cakes. Serve immediately.

CALAMARI

SERVES 6 TO 8

*T*he *American Heritage Dictionary* defines "calamari" simply as "squid prepared as food." The word is Italian, but this simple preparation is found throughout the Mediterranean.

Squid must be cooked either very quickly or very slowly; otherwise they'll be rubbery. I like to grill larger ones, but fresh tiny squid are delicious when simply fried. Serve these as an appetizer, with lemon wedges alongside.

If you can get tiny squid (smaller than 3 inches), you won't even have to clean them, though many people do anyway. Remove the ink sac and quill from small squid (3 to 5 inches). The bodies of medium squid (5 to 8 inches) should be sliced into rings. (Don't fry squid any bigger than these.)

3 pounds fresh squid, as small as possible, cleaned (see box)
Olive oil for deep-frying
Salt and freshly ground black pepper, to taste
1 cup all-purpose flour

1. Cut the bodies of larger squid into ½-inch rings. Make sure the squid have been rinsed and patted as dry as possible.

2. Preheat the oven to 200°F. Place a wire rack on a baking sheet and set it in the oven.

3. Pour oil to a depth of 3 inches in a stockpot or Dutch oven, place it over medium-high

CLEANING SQUID

*T*o clean squid, pull the head away from the body. Most of the entrails will come out with the head. Squeeze the head to force out the hard mouth and beak. Cut the tentacles from the head, just in front of the eyes. Remove the plastic-like quill from the body and discard it. Then squeeze out any remaining viscera from the body and rinse well. Some people peel the skin off the body, but I never do. Pat the squid absolutely dry (or oil will splatter all over the cooking area).

heat, and heat it to 365°F. Salt and pepper the squid. Place the flour in a shallow bowl.

4. When the oil reaches 365°F, drop several pieces of squid into the flour and toss them around to coat them fully. Shake off any excess flour, and then fry them in the hot oil until lightly browned, about 3 minutes. Using a wire mesh strainer, transfer the squid to the wire rack. Continue frying, always maintaining the temperature and not crowding the pot. Serve immediately.

SEARED SCALLOPS

SERVES 4 TO 6

I love scallops, but in restaurants they're so often overcooked that I seldom order them. Instead, I wait until I find really big, beautiful sea scallops, so fresh that they're sticky, and cook them at home. I sear them in a hot pan so that the outsides form a crusty brown surface and the interiors are succulent, just barely cooked. Then I add them, either still warm or cooled, to a salad, drizzled with a favorite vinaigrette. Or sometimes I prepare a pasta sauce and add the scallops to the dish at the last minute so that they won't cook any more. Be sure to use very fresh sticky scallops in this dish. If they aren't sticky, the outsides will not brown.

Twenty-four scallops is plenty to make salads for six; one of my favorite ones includes slices of fennel, orange, and red onion. As part of a pasta dish, allow six scallops per person.

About 1 teaspoon olive oil
24 very fresh jumbo sea scallops (about
   1½ pounds)
Salt and freshly ground black pepper,
   to taste

1. Brush the bottom of a large heavy skillet with a film of olive oil, and place it over high heat. Season the scallops with salt and pepper.

2. When the oil is just beginning to smoke, add the scallops to the skillet and sear them, about 30 seconds on each side. Transfer the scallops to a plate, cover them, and keep them warm while you prepare the rest of your dish (see headnote). Or place them immediately in the refrigerator to chill.

FRIED CLAMS

SERVES 6

I seldom fry clams because most of our local littlenecks and cherrystones are shipped north. And this far south we rarely see real frying clams, which are shucked soft-shells (also known as longnecks or steamers). But when I do find them, I buy a couple of pounds and invite some friends over for what seems a rare treat to us Southerners. If you're a New Englander, you should have no trouble finding frying clams. If you live elsewhere, buy the smallest, freshest clams you can find and shuck them at the last moment. Serve these with lemon wedges, Tartar Sauce, or Red Rémoulade (see Index).

2 pounds freshly shucked frying clams, preferably soft-shells, or 5 pounds small clams in the shell, shucked

1 large egg

1 cup milk

1 cup fine dry bread crumbs

1 teaspoon salt

¼ teaspoon cayenne pepper

Peanut oil for deep-frying

1. Pick over the clams for any pieces of shell, and place them in a bowl. Beat the egg into the milk and pour it over the clams, making sure all the clams are covered. In a shallow bowl, mix the bread crumbs, salt, and cayenne together.

2. Pour oil to a depth of 3 inches in a stockpot or Dutch oven, and place it over medium-high heat. When the oil reaches 365°F, lift a batch of clams out of the bowl with a wire mesh strainer, allowing any excess milk to drip off. Place the clams in the crumbs and coat them well, then drop them into the hot oil and fry them until golden brown. Soft-shells will take about 1 minute, littlenecks about 2. Drain them on paper towels, and continue cooking until all the clams are fried. (Maintain the temperature between 365° and 375°F.) Serve immediately.

FRIED SHRIMP

SERVES 2 TO 6

I love fried shrimp, and I've never had better than at the Edisto Motel on the banks of the Edisto River in South Carolina's lush low country, where people stand in line for hours just to eat the delicious fried seafood and to be pampered by the Hickman family. Sisters Zelma Hickman and Doris Cook will tell you that there's no secret to their artful frying—just clean hot grease and fresh local shrimp. Their shrimp are small (more than forty per pound) and they are truly local, caught right offshore from the beach, a few miles down the river. They clean and devein the shrimp but leave the tails intact.

Zelma and Doris make up an egg wash with milk and a little salt and pour it over the shrimp, then let them drain well. The shrimp are rolled in cracker meal, then put in baskets and tossed to remove any excess meal; the resulting coating is delicate and light. The shrimp are fried for just a minute or two. If you're as generous as they are at the Edisto, you'll count on one pound of shrimp per person! Other low country cooks allow half a pound; outside the area, you seldom get more than a third.

Serve these the Edisto way: hot, with Tartar Sauce and Cocktail Sauce, Coleslaw and hushpuppies (all of which you'll find in the Index).

Peanut oil for deep-frying
2 large eggs
1 cup milk
1 teaspoon salt
2 pounds small fresh shrimp, peeled
    and deveined but tails intact
1 cup cracker meal

1. Pour oil to a depth of 3 inches in a stock-pot or Dutch oven, place it over medium-high heat, and heat it to 365°F.

2. While the oil is heating, beat the eggs, milk, and salt together. Place the shrimp in a bowl, and pour the egg mixture over the shrimp, making sure they are well coated. Then drain the shrimp in a colander, shaking it well to remove all excess egg. Place the cracker meal on a plate.

3. When the oil reaches 365°F, roll the shrimp in the cracker meal, then place them in a dry sieve. Shake off the excess meal over the plate. Fry the shrimp, in batches, in the hot oil until golden brown, 1 to 2 minutes. Remove the shrimp from the oil with a wire mesh strainer, and shake off all excess oil. Serve immediately.

COCONUT FRIED SHRIMP

SERVES 3 TO 6

This is one of the most popular recipes in today's restaurants, reflecting the current interest in Pacific Rim and "Floribbean" cooking. I've tried literally dozens of versions, and these, adapted from Steven Raichlen's *Miami Spice,* are the best I've had. Steve serves his with a sauce that combines horseradish, lime juice, and apricot jam. You can purée the Chunky Fruit Salsa (see Index) if you want a dipping sauce or simply serve it alongside as is. If you're serving the shrimp as a main course, serve some rice as well.

Freshly grated coconut transforms this dish. If there is an Indian market where you live, buy a rotary coconut grater; you can grate the meat in a matter of moments. If you can't get your hands on fresh coconut, use frozen unsweetened flaked coconut. Figure on half a pound of shrimp per person if you're serving these as an entrée, one quarter pound for an appetizer. Steven recommends jumbo shrimp but I prefer the more delicate flavor of smaller ones, which I don't devein. If you use larger shrimp, devein them and leave the tails intact.

8 tablespoons (1 stick) unsalted butter, clarified (page 8)
1½ pounds medium to large shrimp (about 50 total), peeled (see headnote)
1 tablespoon fresh lime juice
Salt and freshly ground black pepper, to taste
1 cup all-purpose flour
2 large eggs
1½ cups freshly grated coconut, or 1 package (6 ounces) frozen flaked unsweetened coconut, thawed

1. Pour the clarified butter into a large heavy skillet. (If you are serving rice, you can add the remaining butter culls to it.)

2. Place the shrimp in a large bowl and toss with the lime juice, salt, and pepper. Allow to marinate for 3 to 5 minutes (5 minutes for larger shrimp).

3. Place the flour in a shallow bowl, the eggs in another, and the coconut in a third. Beat the eggs lightly.

4. Place the skillet over medium heat. Dust each shrimp with flour, shaking off the excess. Then dip it in the egg and allow any excess to drain off. Finally, dip it in the coconut, coating it well. Cook the shrimp in the butter until golden brown, about 1 minute on each side. Drain on paper towels and serve hot.

UPPERLINE'S FRIED GREEN TOMATOES WITH SHRIMP REMOULADE

SERVES 8

This recipe has been copied all over New Orleans, and with good reason, but I first saw it at JoAnn Clevenger's marvelous Upperline restaurant, where updated Creole classics share the menu with traditional and bistro fare. JoAnn's shrimp are peeled before they're boiled; they are both unusual and delicious. The rémoulade sauce is a red one, New Orleans style.

For the tomatoes, try to find rock-hard, blemish-free green tomatoes with no red whatsoever. Fry them in a very small amount of vegetable or light olive oil. JoAnn simply uses buttermilk to dip her green tomatoes; you can also use an egg-and-milk mixture. Either way works fine.

This recipe serves eight, but you can cook it in batches and offer individual servings as they are ready.

FOR THE SHRIMP
3 pounds medium shrimp in the shell
½ cup dry white wine
2 cups water
1 small white onion, peeled
1 bay leaf
1 rib celery
½ teaspoon cayenne pepper
6 peppercorns

FOR THE TOMATOES
¼ cup vegetable or light olive oil,
  or more as needed
1 cup buttermilk, or 1 large egg
  beaten into 1 cup milk

1 cup cornmeal
Salt and freshly ground black pepper,
  to taste
16 slices (½ to ¾ inch thick) green
  tomato (4 to 5 medium tomatoes)
Red Rémoulade (page 163)

1. Peel the shrimp and set them aside, reserving the shells. Place the shrimp shells and all the remaining shrimp ingredients in a saucepan. Bring to a boil, reduce the heat, and cook at a low boil for 30 minutes.

2. Prepare a bowl or sink of ice water.

3. Remove the stock from the heat, strain out the solids, and return the stock to the saucepan. Bring it to a boil. Add the peeled shrimp and simmer for 1 to 2 minutes, cooking until they are just done (until they are no longer translucent). Do not overcook. Strain out the shrimp (reserving the stock for use in a soup), and plunge them into the ice water to stop the cooking. Drain the shrimp, and place them in a covered container in the refrigerator. The shrimp can be cooked up to a day ahead of time.

4. If you plan to serve all eight portions at the same time, preheat the oven to its lowest setting. Place a wire rack on a baking sheet and put it in the oven.

5. Heat ¼ cup oil in a heavy sauté pan over medium heat. Pour the buttermilk into a shallow bowl. In another shallow bowl, combine the cornmeal with the salt and pepper. Dip each tomato slice into the buttermilk and then into the cornmeal, coating the slice well and shaking off any excess. Add as many tomato slices to the pan as will fit, and cook them slowly until golden brown on the bottom, about 2 minutes. Turn the slices and brown on the other side, another 2 minutes. Transfer the cooked tomatoes to the wire rack to keep warm in the oven while you fry the remaining slices. You may have to wipe out the pan between batches; if so, you will have to add more oil.

6. For each serving, place two slices of tomato on each plate, top each slice with three or four chilled shrimp, and top them with 1½ to 2 tablespoons rémoulade.

CHAPTER 5

POULTRY AND MEATS

Many meats must be quickly cooked—or they should be slowly braised. For those of you looking for quickly prepared meats, frying is certainly the way to go. And if you're fond of grilled steaks (and are one of those lucky people who, like me, has little fear of fat), try searing them in a dry skillet instead. You'll not lose the delicious fat that carries flavor.

This chapter provides an overview to the basic types of poultry and meat frying. In addition to the American classics—fried chicken, Smothered Steak, and pork chops—there are international favorites such as Wiener Schnitzel and Empanadas, as well as a handful of dishes prepared with variety meats. These are among the easiest recipes in this book.

Rabbit can be used in many dishes designed for chicken. It's one of those meats that takes well to slow braising or to quick frying because, like many cuts of game and sinewy meat, rabbit has little fat.

REAL SOUTHERN DEEP-FRIED CHICKEN

SERVES 2 DEVOTEES
OR 4 SNACKERS

If you're going to eat the chicken at room temperature, try this simple deep-frying method. The meat will stay crispy longer. Lard is traditional, but you can use peanut oil. I'm not about to say how many people one little chicken will feed, but if you fry only one, you'll not have leftovers.

What many people do not know about fried chicken (and other fried foods) is that the finished dish can be wrapped well, frozen, and refried to heat it up later. For refrying, use a vegetable oil with a high smoke point, such as peanut oil. Preheat the oil to between 390° and 400°F. Then carefully lower the pieces into the oil, frying them until just warmed through, 1 or 2 minutes. Don't let the oil go below 365° or above 400°F.

1 fryer chicken (2½ to 3 pounds), cut
    into 8 to 10 pieces, with skin
Lard or peanut oil for deep-frying
1 cup all-purpose flour
1 teaspoon salt
1 teaspoon freshly ground
    black pepper
¼ teaspoon cayenne pepper or
    paprika

1. Wash the chicken inside and out with cold water, drain it well, and pat it completely dry. (If the chicken is freshly butchered, you can soak it for up to 2 hours in ice water to help draw the blood out.) Put enough lard in a large heavy pot to totally cover the chicken pieces (they should float in the fat). Place the pot over medium-high heat, and heat it to 370°F. Place a wire rack on a baking sheet and set it aside.

2. Combine the flour, salt, black pepper, and cayenne in a heavy paper bag and shake to mix. Add the chicken pieces one at a time, shaking to coat.

3. When the fat reaches 370°F, use tongs to lower the chicken into

the fat, one piece at a time. Do not crowd the pot, and keep the temperature between 365° and 375°F. Fry the chicken until it is golden brown and tender, turning the pieces, if necessary, so they brown evenly, about 20 minutes.

As they are done, transfer the pieces to the wire rack. Use a slotted spoon or a wire mesh strainer to remove any debris from the fat; then continue frying the rest of the chicken. Serve hot, warm, or at room temperature.

SOUTHERN FRIED CHICKEN

As a Southerner, I often ate fried chicken growing up. I knew what home-fried chicken was like long before the Colonel was a household word. At its best, fried chicken is tender, succulent, and not at all greasy. The fast-food chains actually do a good job, because they use clean, very hot, deep fat to fry the chicken so that each piece is totally surrounded by the cooking medium at all times. Deep-fried chicken is the crispest and therefore the best to take on a picnic or to eat at room temperature.

When I lived in the Caribbean, roadside vendors would put a Dutch oven filled with fat onto a charcoal fire. They threw in some whole garlic bulbs, and when the papery garlic skin

browned and the bulb floated to the surface, they added unadorned chicken legs to the pot and cooked them until they too were golden brown and floated freely in the hot fat. It was one of many delicious variations on fried chicken that I've had in my travels.

There are no secrets to fried chicken. *The Savannah Cookbook* of 1933 tells it best, and quite simply: "Cut up the chicken, sprinkle liberally with salt and pepper, dredge with flour, and fry in deep, and very hot, fat." If you watch the process at most of the fast-food chains, that's about all there is to it. At Kentucky Fried Chicken, the quick cooking ("original recipe") is done in a pressure cooker, making for a very juicy bird. The Colonel's claim to eleven secret herbs and spices was debunked in William Poundstone's 1983 book, *Big Secrets*: A laboratory hired by

(continued)

(continued)

Poundstone found only flour, salt, pepper, and MSG in the famous seasoning! You can fry chicken in a pressure cooker if you want to; it will only take ten minutes. You can also deep-fry or pan-fry the chicken.

Most recipes for fried chicken are similar. The chicken pieces—sometimes soaked, sometimes not—are covered with some type of coating (more often than not a dry one), then fried in hot oil until golden brown all over. Some people cover the pan when frying in shallow fat; others don't. Gravy is a given, not the exception. Abby Fisher, a former slave, wrote in her 1881 cookbook, *What Mrs. Fisher Knows About Old Southern Cooking,* "The chicken is done when the fork passes easily into it. After the chicken is all cooked, leave a little of the hot fat in the skillet; then take a tablespoon of dry flour and brown it in the fat, stirring it around, then pour water in and stir till the gravy is as thin as soup."

Thirty-five years before Mrs. Fisher's book appeared, Sarah Rutledge had offered several recipes for fried chicken in *The Carolina Housewife.* Her aristocratic Charleston kitchen offered a more elegant sauce than Mrs. Fisher's gravy: "Skim carefully the gravy in which the chickens have been fried; mix with it half a pint of cream; season with a little mace, pepper and salt, adding some parsley." Another version called "Cold Fried Chicken" called for skinning the chicken, then rubbing it "with an egg beaten up, and cover it with grated bread, seasoned with pepper, salt, and chopped parsley. Fry it in butter; thicken a little brown gravy with flour and butter, and add a little cayenne, pickle, and mushroom ketchup."

I'm not one to mess with tradition too much, especially when that tradition is as delicious as fried chicken. I've included tried-and-true methods here, but don't think these are the only authentic recipes. You can soak the bird or not. You can cover the pan when shallow-frying or not. And these are just the southern U. S. methods. The Chinese, Italians, West Indians, Austrians, Japanese, and Greeks are adept chicken fryers as well.

REAL SOUTHERN PAN-FRIED CHICKEN AND GRAVY

SERVES 2 TO 4

This pan-frying technique, which calls for covering the pan during part of the frying time, is common throughout the South. It makes for a very moist bird, but I recommend it only as a hot meal. Pan-frying recipes often call for soaking birds in buttermilk, but culinary scholar Karen Hess has pointed out that yogurt thinned with a little milk is closer in flavor to the 19th century's clabbered milk and real buttermilk than is today's cultured variety. Serve this with mashed potatoes or rice, but don't put the gravy on the chicken!

Because some pieces of the chicken are larger than others, I fry the chicken at a lower temperature than normal, so that the larger pieces don't burn on the outside before they finish cooking.

1 fryer chicken (2½ to 3 pounds),
    cut into 8 to 10 pieces, with skin
2½ cups milk
¾ cup plain yogurt
2½ cups (about 1 pound) lard or
    peanut oil
Salt and freshly ground black pepper
¼ teaspoon cayenne pepper or
    paprika (optional)
1 cup all-purpose flour
1 small onion, grated
    (1 to 2 tablespoons)

1. Wash the chicken in cold water and drain it well. Place the chicken in a nonreactive bowl or glass baking dish. Mix enough of the milk into the yogurt to make it the consistency of thick cream; it should take about ½ cup. Pour the mixture over the chicken, making sure all the pieces are coated. Set aside for 1 hour.

2. Meanwhile, preheat the oven to 200°F. Set a wire rack on a baking sheet and place it in the oven.

3. Place the chicken pieces in a colander to drain. Put the lard in a deep heavy skillet or sauté pan, place it over medium-high heat,

and heat it to 350°F. Combine 1 teaspoon salt, 1 teaspoon black pepper, the cayenne, and flour in a heavy paper bag. Shake to mix.

4. As the oil approaches 350°F, remove the pieces of chicken from the colander one at a time, shaking off any excess liquid, and add them to the bag, shaking well to coat. Reserve the leftover flour.

5. When the fat reaches 350°F, place the chicken pieces in the pan, one at a time, skin side down. Start with the dark pieces, which take a little longer. Cook in batches, if necessary; you do not want to crowd the chicken, and the oil should come up around the edges of each piece. Cover the pan, reduce the heat a little (you want to keep the temperature at 350°F), and fry for about 5 to 7 minutes, until the underside is brown. Turn the chicken, cover the pan again, and fry for another 5 to 7 minutes. Remove the cover and continue cooking, until the chicken is perfectly crisp and cooked through, about 15 minutes more.

Transfer the chicken to the wire rack to drain and keep warm while you fry the rest and make the gravy.

6. Carefully pour all but 2 or 3 tablespoons of the fat out of the skillet (into any empty juice or milk carton), leaving all the little browned bits in the pan. Place the pan back on the stove over medium heat. Add 2 tablespoons of the reserved flour to the fat, whisking it in and stirring constantly until it begins to brown. Slowly add the remaining 2 cups of milk and the onion and continue cooking, stirring often, until the desired consistency is reached, about 5 minutes. Taste the gravy, add salt and pepper to taste, and pour into a gravy boat to serve.

CHICKEN KIEV

SERVES 2 TO 4

This is one of those old "gourmet" dishes from days gone by: a skinned and boned chicken breast stuffed with a piece of chilled sweet butter and deep-fried to a golden brown. When you cut into the breast, the butter bursts from the chicken. The recipe is Ukrainian, but French, Italian, and American cooks have been making variations of it for decades. If you use ordinary grocery-store chicken, the flavor will be bland. I use organically raised free-range chicken breasts, and add some herbs and garlic to the butter.

Traditionally the dish is accompanied by fresh peas and fried potatoes, but you can serve it with the vegetables of your choice. Hearty diners will eat two breast halves; most people these days will eat just one.

6 tablespoons (¾ stick) unsalted butter, at room temperature
1 teaspoon chopped fresh chives
1 teaspoon fresh thyme leaves
1 clove garlic, minced
4 skinless, boneless chicken breast halves (3 to 4 ounces each)
Salt and freshly ground black pepper, to taste
½ cup all-purpose flour
2 large eggs
1½ cups fine dry bread crumbs
Peanut oil for deep-frying

1. About 4 hours before you plan to serve the dish, mix the butter with the chives, thyme, and garlic. Divide it into four equal parts and shape them into logs about the size of your thumb. Wrap the butter logs in wax paper, and place it in the freezer for about 15 minutes.

2. Place a breast half, smooth side up, on a sheet of wax paper. Place another sheet of wax paper over it and pound the breast with a flat mallet or a rolling pin until it is uniformly thick and about 8 inches long and 5 inches wide. Remove the wax paper and season the breast with salt and pepper. Turn the breast half over and place one of the butter logs on it, about ½ inch in along one long edge. Fold the ends over the butter, and then roll the chicken up to wrap the butter completely. Repeat using the remaining butter and the other three breast halves.

3. Place the flour in a shallow bowl, the eggs in another, and the bread crumbs in another. Beat the eggs well, so that no white is evident. Dip each rolled breast in the flour, then in the egg, and then in the bread crumbs. Place them on a plate and chill, uncovered, in the refrigerator for 3 hours.

4. When you are ready to fry the chicken, pour oil to a depth of 2 to 3 inches in a Dutch oven. The oil should be deeper than the rolled breasts. Place it over medium-high heat, and heat it to 365°F.

5. When the oil reaches 365°F, use tongs to carefully lower the rolls into the oil, and fry them until golden brown, about 5 minutes. Remove them carefully with the tongs, pat dry with paper towels, if necessary, and serve.

FRIED TACOS WITH SHREDDED CHICKEN

MAKES 16; SERVES 4 TO 6

These little tubes of corn tortillas rolled around shredded meat are called *flautas* (flutes) or *taquitos* (little tacos). The recipe is adapted from *Food From My Heart*, by my exuberant Mexican friend Zarela Martinez. Zarela is also the name of her tiny, marvelous restaurant in midtown Manhattan. The stewed chicken is a staple at Zarela; you'll need to make it ahead of time. Buy thin packaged corn tortillas. They fry up nicely.

FOR THE CHICKEN
1 chicken (3½ to 4 pounds)
3 quarts water
2 ribs celery, broken into pieces
2 carrots, broken into pieces
1 large onion, quartered
2 bay leaves
1 sprig of fresh thyme
2 or 3 sprigs of fresh parsley
6 to 10 peppercorns
2 tablespoons lard or olive oil
½ cup finely chopped onion
1 clove garlic, minced
Salt and freshly ground black pepper,
    to taste

FOR THE TACOS
16 corn tortillas
Lard or vegetable oil for deep-frying

Tomatillo Sauce (page 176)

1. Prepare the chicken: Rinse the chicken well and put it in a large stockpot. Add the water, celery, carrots, onion, all the herbs, and peppercorns. Bring almost to a boil. Then reduce the heat and simmer until the meat is just barely cooked through, about 35 minutes. Remove the chicken from the pot. Strain out and discard the rest of the solids. (Save the stock for use in another dish; it can be frozen easily in a large freezer bag or plastic containers.)

2. As soon as the chicken is cool enough to handle, pull off and discard the skin. Using your fingers, pull the meat from the bones and shred it by rubbing it back and forth between your thumb and fingers. You should have about 4 cups of meat. Discard the bones.

3. Add the lard to a large sauté pan and place it over medium heat. When the fat is hot but not smoking, add the onion and garlic and cook, stirring, until the onion is translucent, about 5 minutes. Add 3 cups of the shredded chicken, stirring to mix well with the onion and garlic. Season with salt and pepper, and cook for 5 minutes more, stirring occasionally, so that the flavors can mingle. Remove from the heat and set aside while you prepare the tortillas. (Wrap any remaining chicken tightly and store it in the refrigerator for up to 3 days for use in another recipe.)

4. When you are ready to prepare the tacos, soften the tortillas: Wrap them in a kitchen towel and place it inside a pot fitted with a steamer rack and filled with an inch of water. Cover the pot, bring the water to a boil, and remove it from the heat. Allow it to sit for about 5 minutes. (Zarela says you can also place four tortillas at a time in a small par-tially closed plastic bag and microwave them on full power for 30 to 40 seconds; keep the tortillas in the bag after microwaving.)

5. Don't try to work with more than four tortillas at a time. Working quickly so that the tortillas don't dry out, place about 2 tablespoons of the shredded chicken in the center of each tortilla and roll it up to form a tight cylinder. Secure with a toothpick. As the tortillas are filled, place them in another plastic bag or under a damp towel so that they don't dry out. You can make the tacos up to 6 hours in advance. Place them in a tightly sealed container, on a tray wrapped well with plastic wrap, or in self-seal plastic bags, and store them in the refrigerator.

6. When you are ready to fry the tacos, preheat the oven to 200°F. Place a wire rack on a baking sheet and set it in the oven.

7. Place 2 to 3 inches of lard in a Dutch oven or stockpot over medium heat. When it reaches 365°F, add the tacos (without crowding the pot). Fry until golden brown on both sides, about 5 minutes. Using tongs, transfer them to the wire rack to keep warm while you fry the rest. Serve hot, with the Tomatillo Sauce.

DEEP-FRIED TURKEY

20 SERVINGS

If you live in the South, you've probably heard of deep-frying an entire turkey—it's a new and popular tradition. I first saw it done when I was in high school in the 1960s; Justin Wilson, the Louisiana cookbook author and television personality, says he first did it in Louisiana in the 1930s. I think it appeared in the South simply because it's such an outdoors event—and an *event* it is: a huge (10-gallon) pot sizzles with lots (5 gallons) of oil over a very hot fire. You can't do it indoors. You can cook whole chickens or a turkey breast (page 84) the same way in less oil, but still you mustn't try it indoors: you don't want to risk setting that much oil on fire inside.

Whole fried turkey is the best illustration I know of just how delicious and greaseless fried food can be. I bet that once you've tried it fried, you'll never go back to roast turkey. While the turkey is cooking, take advantage of the big pot of oil to fry something else, like French fries. You can serve the turkey as the center of a big meal, such as Thanksgiving dinner; it will only take about an hour from setup to serving. Or you can have your guests make turkey or club sandwiches, and serve them with fries.

You will need an outdoor cooker (mine is 140,000 Btu) and a 10-gallon pot, preferably one with a basket insert (available in hardware stores and stores where outdoor equipment is sold). The insert keeps the bird off the bottom of the pot and facilitates removing it from the oil.

4 to 5 gallons vegetable oil
1 whole turkey (12 to 15 pounds),
at room temperature
Cayenne pepper (optional)

1. Begin heating the oil in a 10-gallon pot over a very hot propane flame outdoors. Don't set the burner to its highest setting, as you may need to increase the heat after you've added the turkey. It will take about 20 minutes for the oil to heat.

2. Meanwhile, rinse the turkey well, pat it dry inside and out, and set it on end in a sink to drain.

3. When the oil reaches 375°F, pat the turkey dry again, and sprinkle

FRYER BEWARE

There are a few safety tips to keep in mind before frying turkey outdoors. Remember you're dealing with gallons of dangerously hot oil, so make sure there are no kids or pets running around. And you want to wear some old shoes that you can slip out of easily and long pants just in case you do spill some oil on you.

You really want to be careful lowering the bird into and raising it out of the oil; the safest and easiest way is to use a large stockpot with a basket insert. If you can't get a basket insert large enough, do what I do: Use a clean fireplace poker to remove the turkey from the hot oil. Insert the poker into the large cavity of the bird and hook it through the wishbone end of the breast. If you do choose to do it this way, before cooking the turkey, practice the feel of hooking the bird on the kitchen table. You also will need to be strong enough to lift the bird out of the oil (and hold it over the pot for a moment to let the oil drain off) and transfer it to the rack. I've never had an accident, but I am always very cautious.

You'll also want to place the cooker away from shrubs or leaves, and if your cooker has a sturdy base, I do advise placing it on the grass rather than on your patio or deck; spilled grease is easier on the lawn than it is on concrete or wood.

it with cayenne, if desired. If your cooker has a basket insert, place the turkey in the basket and set it over a baking sheet; if not, set an oven rack over a large baking sheet, place the turkey on it, and take them outside to the cooker.

4. Check the temperature of the oil. When the oil reaches 390°F, carefully and slowly lower the basket with the turkey into the oil; or lower it holding it by its legs or by a long heavy tool such as a clean fireplace poker inserted into its cavity. *Be careful!* Immediately check the oil temperature and adjust the flame so that the temperature does not dip below 340°F. You want to maintain the temperature at 365°F. As it cooks, occasionally move the bird around in the oil so that it does not scorch (the oil near the heat source will be hotter).

Whole turkeys take only 3 to 4 minutes per pound to fry to perfection: small ones, around 12 pounds, will take about 35 minutes; large ones, around 15 pounds, will take about 1 hour. When it is done, the turkey will float to the surface with a perfectly crispy, brown skin. If you are unsure, you can test the meat for doneness at the hip joint or insert a meat thermometer into the breast; it should register 180°F.

5. Using the basket insert if there is one, or by again inserting a long heavy tool such as a clean fireplace poker into its cavity, carefully remove the turkey from the oil and hold it over the pot for a moment to allow any excess oil to drain back into the pot, then lay the bird on the oven rack. Allow it to rest for 20 minutes before carving.

DEEP-FRIED TURKEY BREAST

6 TO 8 SERVINGS

You can enjoy the wonderful flavor of deep-fried turkey by cooking the breast only, but this remains strictly an outdoors project. Before you begin frying the turkey, make sure you have read the box on frying safety on page 83.

2 gallons vegetable oil
1 fresh bone-in turkey breast (about 5 pounds), at room temperature
Cayenne pepper (optional)

1. In a 5-gallon stockpot, preferably with a basket insert, begin heating the oil outdoors over a gas burner. Don't set the flame to its highest setting, as you may need to increase the heat after you add the turkey breast. Place a wire rack over a baking sheet and set it aside.

2. Pat the breast dry, then sprinkle it all over with cayenne, if desired.

3. When the oil reaches 375°F, slowly and carefully lower the breast into the oil, in the insert basket if available. Fry the breast for 4 to 6 minutes per pound, or until it is evenly golden brown all over and is floating freely in the oil, about 25 minutes. A meat thermometer inserted carefully into the thickest part of the breast will register 180°F when the breast is fully cooked.

4. Carefully remove the breast from the oil and hold it over the pot for a moment so that any excess oil can drain away. Place the breast on the wire rack and allow it to cool for 15 minutes before carving.

SEARED DUCK BREASTS

Duck is my favorite meat, and while I love the crunchy skin and the rich meat of a roast bird, I most often cook the breast, which I prefer rare, in a skillet. I simmer the rest of the body with aromatics or I make confit, a marvelous dish from southwestern France that preserves the duck by cooking it and storing it in its own fat.

Duck begs for fruity sauces. You can serve these seared breasts with a fruit chutney, or simply deglaze the pan with some blackberry vinegar and throw in a few fresh berries—or use apple cider and a few apple slices. Or you can add some parboiled vegetables such as potatoes or green beans to the delicious fat after the breast is cooked, stir-frying them quickly with some garlic to warm them through. Duck breasts cooked in a skillet should be served medium to rare, but you'll want the skin to be crisp.

Sprinkle both sides of boned breast halves with salt, freshly ground black pepper, and cayenne pepper, to taste. Place them on a plate or platter, cover them with plastic wrap, and place in the refrigerator to chill thoroughly. About 20 minutes before you're ready to serve the duck, heat a heavy skillet over medium-high heat until it is very hot. A drop of water will vaporize instantly when the pan's ready. Remove the chilled breasts from the refrigerator and pour off any liquid that has drained from them. Place the breast halves skin side down in the pan. Immediately reduce the heat to medium-low and allow the fat to render out of the skin. If you're not going to add other ingredients to the pan, you can pour off the fat as it renders out, but be sure to save it for another use; it's delicious! Leave the breast skin side down until all of the fat has rendered out and the skin is perfectly crisp and golden brown. It will take about 15 minutes. At this point you can remove the duck breasts and continue the cooking later.

If you are continuing with the cooking now, turn the breasts over and cook them until they are done to your liking. Ducks vary widely in the size of their breasts. It's best to learn to judge whether the meat is done by touch: quickly press the thick end of the breast with your finger to see how springy the meat feels; the springier it is, the more done it is. It will take about 4 or 5 minutes for rare to medium rare. When done, remove the duck from the pan and allow it to sit for about 2 minutes before you carve it, cutting the meat at an angle and fanning it out on the dinner plate for an attractive presentation.

PAN-SEARED STEAKS WITH MUSHROOMS

SERVES 2

Dry-frying a steak in a cast-iron skillet is a perfect way to cook it; I prefer this technique to grilling. Working quickly, you'll produce perfectly rare, delicious steaks. Just be sure to use tongs rather than a fork to turn the steaks: you don't want to pierce the meat. Mushrooms and onions are added to the pan drippings here, and a little red wine rounds the flavors. The recipe feeds two, but you can multiply it for more people. Serve the steaks with Pan-Fried Potatoes (see Index).

2 well-marbled boneless strip steaks
    (each about 1 inch thick and weighing
    ½ pound) of prime or choice beef
Coarsely ground black pepper
2 tablespoons unsalted butter
1 cup chopped onions
¼ pound mushrooms, preferably
    shiitakes, stems discarded, caps
    sliced thick or left whole if small
Spicy young red Rhône wine, such as
    Côtes du Rhône

1. Remove the steaks from the refrigerator at least 30 minutes before you plan to cook them to bring them to room temperature.

2. Preheat the oven to its lowest setting and place two dinner plates in it.

3. Place a large cast-iron skillet over high heat and get it very hot (a drop of water will vaporize instantly when the pan's ready). Pepper the steaks well on both sides, and add them to the skillet as soon as it's hot. Cook the steaks for 1½ to 2 minutes, then shake the pan. (Be careful; this pan is hot.) They should be seared enough to loosen. Turn down the heat a bit, and turn the steaks over. Cook for 2 minutes on the second side, shake the pan again to loosen them, and transfer them to the warm plates in the oven.

4. Immediately put the butter, onions, and mushrooms in the pan. Cook, shaking the pan often, until the mushrooms have given off most of their juice. Pour yourself a glass of wine and remove the steaks from the oven. Splash some of the wine (about ¼ cup) into the pan and, as it bubbles, stir once or twice with a wooden spoon to loosen any browned bits on the bottom of the pan. Spoon the sauce over the steaks, which should be rare if cooked for the specified amount of time, and serve immediately, along with the rest of the wine.

SMOTHERED STEAK

SERVES 4

S mothered steak is a pan-fried steak. It's known as "chicken-fried" steak in Texas and "country-fried" in the Piedmont and mountain South. It's called "smothered" in the Deep South because it's always served with a peppery gravy made from the pan drippings. It's traditionally made with the tougher cuts of meat, such as a round of beef or venison, well pounded to tenderize it. Many grocers today sell machine-perforated cuts of "cube" steak, which work fine with this recipe. Serve this with Mashed Potatoes or Steamed Rice to soak up the gravy.

¼ cup peanut oil
¼ cup all-purpose flour
4 cube steaks, or 4 beef or venison
    steaks pounded with a mallet
    (1 pound in all)
Salt and freshly ground black pepper,
    to taste
1 cup water or milk
Mashed Potatoes or Steamed Rice
    (pages 188 and 183)

1. Heat the oil in a heavy skillet over medium-high heat. Place a wire rack on a baking sheet and set it aside. Place four dinner plates in the oven and set it to its lowest heat.

2. Place the flour in a shallow bowl. Season the steaks with salt and pepper; then dust them on both sides with the flour, shaking off any excess (reserve the leftover flour). Fry the steaks in the oil until well browned, 1 to 2 minutes per side. Place them on the wire rack to drain while you make the gravy.

3. Pour off the oil but leave the browned bits in the skillet. Reduce the heat and add the leftover flour (you should have 2 or 3 tablespoons) to the skillet, stirring constantly. Add the water and continue stirring over medium-low heat until you have a rich gravy, about 5 minutes. Correct the seasoning with salt and lots of black pepper.

4. Remove the warmed plates from the oven, and divide the steaks and Mashed Potatoes among them. Pour the gravy over all, and serve immediately.

STIR-FRIED BEEF WITH GREEN BEANS

SERVES 2 TO 4

Stir-frying is one of the easiest ways to cook. This recipe can be used as a blueprint for other meals. What's important is to cut the meat and vegetables into small, uniform pieces so that they cook quickly and evenly. You can serve this dish hot with rice as the main course after a clear soup and Spring Rolls (see Index), or you can chill it and serve it as a salad.

FOR THE MARINADE AND BEEF

1 tablespoon soy sauce

1 tablespoon dry sherry

1 clove garlic, minced

1 teaspoon grated fresh ginger

1 tablespoon sesame oil or chile sesame oil or ½ teaspoon hot red pepper flakes

½ pound flank steak, thinly sliced on the diagonal, or ½ pound sirloin, thinly sliced

TO FINISH

3 tablespoons peanut oil

½ pound fresh young green beans, with the stem end trimmed but the fresh young tip intact

3 scallions, white part and a little of the green, cut diagonally into ½-inch pieces

½ cup sliced water chestnuts

1½ teaspoons cornstarch

1 tablespoon beef bouillon or water

1. To marinate the beef, mix the soy sauce, sherry, garlic, ginger, and sesame oil or red pepper flakes together in a shallow container. Add the sliced meat and toss to distribute evenly. Set aside for 30 minutes at room temperature.

2. To finish the dish, heat the peanut oil in a wok over medium-high heat. When it is hot but not smoking, add the green beans and stir-fry, stirring, until they begin to barely change color or soften, 1 to 4 minutes, depending on their age. Add the meat and its marinade, and continue to stir-fry for about 2 minutes

more; the meat should still be pink. Add the scallions and water chestnuts and toss well, evenly distributing the ingredients. Mix the cornstarch with the bouillon and immediately add it to the wok, continuing to stir. Allow the liquid to come to a boil, then swirl it around in the wok until it thickens. Remove from the heat and serve immediately.

EMPANADAS

MAKES 12 EMPANADAS; SERVES 4 AS A MAIN COURSE

Savory meat-filled turnovers are known throughout the world. I've had fiery hot meat patties in the West Indies (but for their seasoning of Scotch bonnet peppers, they were the same as these empanadas). In Galicia, in northwestern Spain, I had little turnovers that had been baked early in the day, served at room temperature at a tapas bar. I like these Latin American turnovers best served hot for lunch or made into smaller pies as finger food for a party.

You can make the empanadas ahead of time and chill them before frying, or you can make them while the oil preheats and fry them as soon as they are made.

2½ cups self-rising flour
Salt
½ cup lard or unsalted butter (1 stick), chilled
½ cup ice water
1 tablespoon olive oil
½ pound ground beef sirloin
½ cup chopped onion
1 clove garlic, minced
½ teaspoon hot red pepper flakes
¼ teaspoon ground cumin
Freshly ground black pepper, to taste
Peanut oil for deep-frying

1. Sift the flour and ½ teaspoon salt together into a large mixing bowl with slanting sides. Cut the lard into small pieces, and add them to the flour. Work the fat into the flour with a pastry blender or two knives. When it is incorporated uniformly, drizzle the ice water into the mixture, tossing with a fork as you do so. Pick up the dough, which will be

crumbly, in your hands and form it into a ball. Wrap the dough well in plastic wrap or wax paper, and refrigerate it for at least 30 minutes and up to several hours.

2. Make the filling: Place the olive oil in a large heavy skillet over medium-high heat and swirl it around to coat the bottom of the pan. Add the meat and cook, stirring to break up any clumps, until lightly browned, about 5 minutes. Add the onion, garlic, red pepper flakes, and cumin. Cook, stirring, until the onions begin to become translucent, 4 to 5 minutes more. Season with salt and pepper. Remove the filling from the pan, and place it in the refrigerator to cool.

3. If you will be cooking the empanadas right away, pour oil to a depth of 3 to 4 inches in a stockpot or Dutch oven, place it over medium-high heat, and heat it to 375°F.

4. While the oil is heating, prepare the empanadas: Remove the dough and filling from the refrigerator. Cut the dough in half, rewrapping one of the halves and placing it back in the refrigerator. On a lightly floured surface, roll out the other half to form a rough rectangle. Fold each of the sides in toward the middle so that you have square corners. Then roll the dough out to form an 8 × 12-inch rectangle. With a knife, slice the rectangle into six 4-inch

squares. Place a heaping tablespoon of filling in the center of each square; then paint a ¼-inch band of water along two of the adjacent edges of the square. Then, fold the opposite corner over to form a triangular turnover, lining the edges up perfectly. To seal the edges well, press with the tines of a fork. Repeat with the second half of the dough and the remaining filling. If you're frying the pies immediately, monitor the temperature of the oil while you're making the empanadas. It should not go over 375°F. (If you are going to fry the empanadas at a later time, use a metal spatula to carefully transfer them to a baking sheet, cover with plastic wrap, and refrigerate them for up to 6 hours.)

5. When you are ready to fry the empanadas, place some crumpled paper towels in a colander. When the oil reaches 375°F, fry three empanadas at a time, keeping the oil above 365°F. (If you are frying chilled empanadas, heat the oil to 390°F and do not let it drop below 370°F.) Fry the empanadas until they are golden brown all over, about 3 minutes. Use a wire mesh strainer to carefully lower and raise the turnovers. Remove the empanadas, letting any excess oil drip back into the pot, and then place them on the paper towels to drain. Repeat the process with the remaining turnovers. Serve immediately.

WIENER SCHNITZEL

SERVES 4

Some food writers say that this is a French dish, but it is so culturally rooted in Austria that I can think of nothing more Viennese than these breaded veal cutlets. It's really not much of a recipe; it's mostly a matter of timing and technique. Any general cookbook will give you instructions for the French version, which is sautéed in lemon butter; this is the real thing.

Some Viennese cooks serve these cutlets with an anchovy sauce; others recommend nothing but lemon. All insist on lard as the proper frying medium, though you may use oil. If the veal is beautifully cut, it shouldn't require pounding. However, you do want the cutlets to have a perfectly even thickness. I simply press a cast-iron skillet down firmly on the cutlets. A green salad is the perfect accompaniment.

4 veal cutlets (each about ¼ inch thick
**   and weighing ¼ pound)**
Salt and freshly ground black pepper,
**   to taste**
¼ cup all-purpose flour
1 large egg, beaten
½ cup fine dry bread crumbs
Lard or peanut oil for frying
**   (about 1½ cups)**
Lemon wedges, for serving

1. Cut a few incisions around the edges of each cutlet and place them between two pieces of wax paper. Place a cast-iron skillet on the paper and press firmly so that the meat is evenly thick. Remove and discard the wax paper. Pat the cutlets dry, then season them lightly with salt and pepper. Place the flour in a shallow dish, the egg in another, and the bread crumbs in a third.

2. Heat the lard to 375°F in a deep skillet or Dutch oven over medium-high heat.

3. While the lard is heating, dip each cutlet quickly in the flour, then the egg, then the bread crumbs, shaking off the extra of each. There should be a thin coating of each, but no clumps.

4. When the fat reaches 375°F, very quickly fry the cutlets until lightly golden, about 1 minute on each side. Use tongs to turn them and to remove them from the pot. Pat them dry with paper towels and serve immediately, with lemon wedges alongside.

VEAL SWEETBREADS WITH CHICKEN

4 SERVINGS

This is the classic French pairing of succulent sweetbreads with medallions of chicken breast. The dish can be an elegant springtime lunch with cooked early peas or asparagus added to the sauce at the last minute. Serve it with rice.

You can make your own chicken stock while the sweetbreads are being pressed: use a small fryer chicken, remove its breast for the dish, then prepare the stock with the remainder of the chicken.

¾ **pound veal sweetbreads**

¼ **cup all-purpose flour**

½ **teaspoon salt**

2 **skinless, boneless chicken breast halves (about 5 ounces each), cut into 2-inch medallions**

4 **tablespoons (½ stick) unsalted butter**

⅓ **cup dry white wine**

⅓ **cup homemade chicken stock or canned broth**

¾ **pound fresh early peas or cut-up asparagus, cooked, or 1 package (10 ounces) frozen peas, thawed (optional)**

1. About 4 hours before you plan to eat, soak the sweetbreads in several changes of cold water until the water is no longer cloudy, 30 minutes to 1 hour. Place the sweetbreads in a saucepan and cover with cold water. Bring the water to a simmer and cook for 5 to 6 minutes; then place the sweetbreads in cold

water to cool. Remove the membrane and connective tissues. Wrap the sweetbreads in a dry kitchen towel, place them on a baking sheet, and cover them with a 2- or 3-pound weight for 3 hours in the refrigerator.

2. Heat the oven to its lowest setting, and place a plate in it to warm. Slice the sweetbreads into 2-inch-diameter medallions. In a shallow bowl, mix the flour with the salt. Dust the sweetbread and chicken pieces on both sides with the flour, shaking off any excess.

3. Melt 3 tablespoons of the butter in a skillet or sauté pan over medium heat, and sauté

the sweetbreads until crisp, about 5 minutes per side. Transfer them to the warmed plate in the oven. Sauté the chicken pieces as well, again about 5 minutes per side, and add them to the warmed plate.

4. Pour the wine and stock into the skillet, raise the heat, and deglaze the pan, shaking it and scraping up any little brown pieces that may have stuck to the bottom. Reduce the liquid by half, 5 to 10 minutes. Cut the remaining 1 tablespoon butter into several small pieces, and whisk them into the sauce one piece at a time. If you are adding vegetables to the dish, reduce the heat and add them at this point; allow them to warm thoroughly. Then add the sweetbreads and chicken, and toss gently to glaze them with the sauce. Serve immediately.

LIVER AND ONIONS

SERVES 4

People seem to either love or hate liver. I was in the latter group for years, assuming that all liver dishes were the pale gray overcooked varieties I had sampled in "meat-and-threes"—those lunch counters of downtown America where workers, students, and townsfolk dine on the "meat of the day" and three vegetables for the cost of an appetizer in fancier digs. And then I went to Europe!

Liver and onions are sautéed in butter in France and in olive oil in Italy, but I prefer the old English version, which became America's: with bacon fat. There are just two "secrets" to perfectly delicious liver: buy good-quality liver and avoid overcooking it. If you have access to a butcher, ask him to slice the liver in pieces of even thickness, with no thin ends that will overcook and toughen. Buy veal liver (from a calf less than 3 months old) if you can find it.

Serve Mashed Potatoes or Steamed Rice (see Index) alongside.

¼ cup strained bacon fat
1 pound veal or calf's liver with
    membrane removed, sliced into
    equal pieces about ½ inch thick

Salt and freshly ground black pepper,
    to taste
¾ cup all-purpose flour
4 onions, thinly sliced

1. Preheat the oven to 200°F. Place a serving platter in the oven to stay warm.

2. Place a large heavy skillet over medium-high heat and add the bacon fat. Pat the liver slices dry, and season them on both sides with salt and pepper. Put the flour in a bowl and dredge the liver slices in it, dusting off any excess.

3. When the bacon fat is hot but not yet smoking, add the liver slices to the pan (don't crowd it). Cook until browned on the bottom,

1 to 2 minutes depending on the thickness of the slices. Use tongs to turn them over, and cook until browned on the second side, 1 minute more. Transfer the slices to the warmed platter and fry any remaining slices that didn't fit in the pan.

4. Dump all the onions into the pan at once, and cook them, gently stirring them around, until they are completely limp and have begun to brown, about 7 minutes. Remove the liver from the oven, top with the onions, and serve immediately.

PORK SOUTHWESTERN

SERVES 6

This recipe comes from Charleston chef Scott Fales who, with his wife, Ruth, owns my longtime favorite restaurant, the Pinckney Cafe. The dish features cornmeal-dusted pork tenderloin sautéed with a mildly spicy ancho pepper and onion sauce. Serve it with black beans and rice.

FOR THE BROTH
2 to 3 tablespoons vegetable oil
1 medium onion, chopped
1 carrot, chopped
2 teaspoons whole coriander
    seeds
2 teaspoons whole peppercorns
2 quarts chicken stock, preferably
    homemade

FOR THE ONION-PEPPER SAUCE
8 tablespoons (1 stick) unsalted butter
1 medium onion, chopped
2 ancho chile peppers, seeded and
    julienned
2 to 3 cloves garlic, minced
Grated zest of 1 lemon
2 teaspoons minced fresh cilantro leaves
3 tablespoons soy sauce

FOR THE PORK
1½ pounds pork tenderloin
½ cup stone-ground cornmeal
2 to 3 tablespoons vegetable oil

1. First, prepare the broth: Cover the bottom of a stockpot with a film of oil, and place it over medium-high heat. Add all of the vegetables and spices and cook, stirring occasionally, until the vegetables are browned, about 15 minutes.

2. Add the chicken stock and raise the heat to high. When the stock boils, lower the heat to medium-high and cook at a low boil until the liquid is reduced by half, about 20 minutes. Then strain the broth and discard the solids. The broth can be made in advance and refrigerated or even frozen.

3. Next, prepare the onion-pepper sauce: In a large sauté pan that has a lid, melt 2 tablespoons of the butter over medium heat. Add the onion and cook until it becomes translucent, 5 to 10 minutes.

4. Add the chile peppers and the garlic, reduce the heat to low, cover, and cook for about 20 minutes, or until all the ingredients are limp and the flavors have mingled. Remove the pan from the heat, uncover it, and stir in the lemon zest and cilantro.

5. If your sauté pan will hold all of the ingredients, you can use it for the final preparation of the sauce. If not, you'll have to transfer the onions and peppers to a saucepan. Add the remaining 6 tablespoons butter, the soy sauce, and the prepared broth. Cook over high heat until the sauce is thick enough to coat the back of a spoon, 10 to 15 minutes.

6. Meanwhile, prepare the pork: Trim the tenderloin of fat and "silverskin" covering the outside of the meat. Cut it into 12 medallions. Pat each medallion with the palm of your hand or the flat side of a knife blade to form an attractive 2½-inch tournedos.

7. Place six plates in the oven and preheat it to 200°F. Place the cornmeal in a shallow bowl. Cover the bottom of a large sauté pan with oil, and place it over medium-high heat. Dust the pork medallions on both sides with the cornmeal, shaking off any excess.

8. Sauté the pork medallions in batches until browned, about 2 minutes on each side. As the medallions are done, transfer them to the warmed plates in the oven. Wipe out the sauté pan after each batch and add fresh oil to cover bottom of the pan, and repeat until all the medallions are browned. Nap the pork with the sauce, and serve immediately.

PAN-FRIED PORK CHOPS

SERVES 4

Pork chops can be greasy and tough if they are fried too long. The secret is to fry them quickly in hot oil, taking them out of the pan the instant they're done. I like to use cracker meal as a coating, but be careful of the ingredients in packaged meals. Martha White Foods (see Sources, page 189) produces a meal that is 100 percent flour; it's the best I've found.

I always serve these chops with beans, such as butter beans or black-eyed peas, rice, and cornbread. In the summer, add some sliced ripe tomatoes.

Peanut oil for frying
4 bone-in pork chops, each about ¾ inch thick (and weighing ½ pound)
Salt and freshly ground black pepper, to taste
½ cup cracker meal (see headnote)

1. Pour oil to a depth of about ¾ inch in a heavy skillet or sauté pan, place it over medium-high heat, and heat it to 365°F.

2. While the oil is heating, put two paper towels on a work surface, place the pork chops on them, and pat them dry with another paper towel. Then season the chops with salt and pepper. Turn the chops over to the other side, placing them on a clean part of the paper towels. Pat dry and season to taste. Put the cracker meal in a paper bag.

3. When the oil reaches 365°F, put the chops in the bag, one at a time, and shake well to coat with the meal. Gently place each chop in the skillet and fry (maintaining a temperature between 365° and 375°F) until golden brown, about 4 minutes on each side. Using tongs, remove the chops in the order that they were placed in the pan, holding each one over the pan so that any excess oil drips back into the pan. Place the chops on clean paper towels and pat dry. Serve immediately.

CROQUETTES

MAKES 8 CROQUETTES; SERVES 4 AS A MAIN COURSE

Here's a basic recipe for croquettes made with cooked meat. Serve these for dinner with a tomato sauce or with side dishes of rice and greens. You can make the mixture the night before or early in the day; it needs to chill before frying. If you deep-fry them, scoop up balls with an ice-cream scoop. For pan-frying, you can simply form patties. Mrs. Fisher (see box, page 98) says to make "cakes as you would a biscuit, round."

Season these to suit your own palate. With chicken, I recommend thyme or lemon thyme; oregano complements lamb. Parsley goes well with any meat. Use a little hot pepper sauce or cayenne if the croquettes are made from ham; add some garlic to beef.

FOR THE FORCEMEAT
1 cup Béchamel Sauce (page 169)
1 tablespoon grated onion
1 tablespoon chopped fresh herbs of
    your choice (see headnote)
1 clove garlic, minced (optional)
2 cups ground or finely chopped
    cooked meat (chicken, beef, veal,
    lamb, ham, etc.)
Salt and freshly ground black pepper,
    to taste
Cayenne pepper, to taste
Hot pepper sauce, to taste

FOR THE CROQUETTES
1 large egg
1 tablespoon water
1 cup all-purpose flour
2 cups fine dry bread crumbs
Peanut oil for frying

1. Prepare the forcemeat: Several hours or the night before you plan to serve the croquettes, combine all the ingredients in a bowl and mix together well, adjusting the seasoning to suit your palate. Cover the bowl and refrigerate.

2. When you are ready to cook the croquettes, place a sheet of wax paper or parchment on a baking sheet. In a shallow bowl, use a whisk to beat the egg with the water. Place the flour in another shallow bowl, and the bread crumbs in a third.

MRS. FISHER'S CROQUETTES

Abby Fisher was an African-American cook of wide renown in Victorian San Francisco, and that city's Women's Co-operative Printing Office published a book of her recipes in 1881. *What Mrs. Fisher Knows About Old Southern Cooking* remained a rare and esoteric piece of American history until it was republished in 1995, with historical notes by the scholar Karen Hess. It is probably the first cookbook written by an African-American. Though we know little of Mrs. Fisher, we now have an amazing collection of recipes that highlight the culinary skills of this cooking legend.

Among the recipes—which are, as Hess points out, "all perfectly lovely, and all perfectly feasible in today's kitchens"— elegant breads, perfectly turned roasts, broiled chops, delicate cakes, and hearty stews share the bill with the preserves for which Mrs. Fisher was well known. (The title page of the book declares that she was twice the winner of medals at the San Francisco Mechanics' Institute Fair for best "Pickles and Sauces and best assortment of Jellies and Preserves.")

She was also an artful fryer, as is evidenced by her "carolas" (crullers), her fried chicken, and her entire chapter of croquettes! "You can make croquettes from any kind of meat you like," she tells us. "You need not use onions unless you like, but always salt and pepper." Her lamb croquettes include a little sour pickle, a brightening flavor for strong-tasting lamb. For her liver croquettes, she instructs, "season high." With a croquette of veal and calf's brains, she suggests serving an elegant sauce of parsleyed cream. What Mrs. Fisher knew was that with a little leftover meat you can make a meal in minutes.

I encourage you to concoct your own meat croquettes. Variety meats, tomato pulp, and béchamel sauce can be included in croquettes as well as the usual egg, mayonnaise, and bread crumbs. Sausage patties are croquettes made of ground meat bound with fat. You can add chopped oysters to sausages and they'll fry up nicely. Sautéed onions, garlic, celery, and peppers, both chile and bell, are nearly always welcome additions.

3. Remove the forcemeat from the refrigerator. Make eight croquettes from the mixture, scooping them up with a large spoon or an ice-cream scoop. You can make classic cone shapes or balls—or patties if you plan to pan-fry them. Dust each croquette on all sides with flour, then dip it in the beaten egg, letting any extra egg drip back into the bowl. Then gently place the croquette in the bread crumbs, coating the entire surface. Place the croquettes on the prepared baking sheet, and set it in the refrigerator to chill while you prepare to fry them.

4. Preheat the oven to 200°F. Place a wire rack on a baking sheet and set it in the oven. If you are deep-frying, pour oil to a depth of 3 inches in a stockpot or Dutch oven, and place it over medium-high heat. If pan-frying, pour oil to a depth of 1 inch in a large heavy skillet or sauté pan, and place it over medium-high heat. Heat the oil to 390°F.

5. When the oil reaches 375°F, remove the croquettes from the refrigerator. When the oil reaches 390°F, add as many croquettes as will fit in the pot without crowding. Be sure to maintain the temperature between 375° and 390°F. Fry the croquettes until golden brown all over, turning them as needed, about 2 minutes. Use a wire mesh strainer to transfer the croquettes to the wire rack, and keep them warm while you fry the remainder. Serve immediately.

FRIED LAMB PATTIES

SERVES 8

These popular Middle Eastern meatballs are called *kibbeh*. Served many ways, from raw to deep-fried, kibbeh is made of finely ground lamb mixed with bulgur and seasoned with onions and spices. (Bulgur is cracked wheat that has been precooked; it is also known as burghul.) *Kibbeh* is a major part of the *mezze*—the vast array of appetizers offered in the Arab states. The amount of bulgur varies widely; in some countries it is omitted.

Tender cuts of lamb, preferably from the leg, are used; the mixture is traditionally pounded in a large mortar until the paste is silken. Call your butcher in advance and have him grind the lamb for you at least three times, very finely on the last grind.

Serve these hot as an appetizer. You can offer lettuce leaves and lemon wedges with them (the lettuce is used to hold them), or you can serve them with Cucumber and Yogurt Salad (see Index), with or without Arabic bread. Fresh mint leaves are the perfect garnish.

1½ cups fine bulgur
1 pound very finely ground tender
  lean lamb
1 large onion, finely grated
1½ teaspoons salt
Freshly ground black pepper,
  to taste
¼ teaspoon ground allspice
1 cup olive oil

1. Soak the bulgur in cold water to cover for about 10 minutes. Then thoroughly drain it in a colander lined with several layers of dampened cheesecloth or a dampened tea towel. Wrap the bulgur in the cheesecloth and squeeze out any excess moisture.

2. Place the bulgur in a large mixing bowl and add the lamb, onion, and all of the seasonings. Wet your hands with cold water and knead the mixture by hand for as long as you can or until the mixture is very smooth. It will take at least 20 minutes. If you have a meat grinder, you can put the *kibbeh* through the grinder several times, using the finest grind. You can also use a large mortar and pestle or a mallet on a large cutting surface to pound the mixture smooth. It should be shiny. Wet your hands or sprinkle a little water into the mixture occasionally; it will help smooth the *kibbeh*.

3. Pour the oil into a large skillet and place it over medium-high heat. Divide the kibbeh into eight equal portions and shape them into burger-like patties. When a haze forms on the oil, fry the *kibbeh* until golden brown all over, about 10 minutes. Remove the patties from the pan and serve at once.

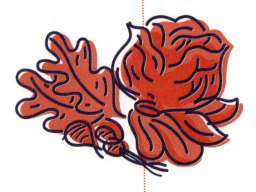

FRIED WONTONS

MAKES ABOUT 50 WONTONS

Fried wontons invite a world of condiments. I like the cross-cultural combination of fried wontons with Chunky Fruit Salsa (see Index); you can put the salsa in a blender and purée it if you like. Any of the traditional Asian dipping sauces (see Index) will work, too. You can, of course, use these for wonton soup: Simply boil the wontons in chicken stock for three or four minutes instead of frying them, garnish with scallions, and serve hot.

Wonton wrappers are widely available in supermarkets today. The Japanese make circular ones called *gyoza* (pot-sticker) skins; they come in 10-ounce packages. Every package of wonton wrappers that I've come across has a basic recipe for the filling as well as instructions for folding the wrapper. These, too, are general instructions—you can vary the filling in any number of ways.

1 package (1 pound) wonton
    wrappers, or 1 package (10 ounces)
    gyoza skins
1 pound fresh spinach, or 1 package
    (10 ounces) frozen spinach,
    thawed and drained
2 teaspoons sake or Chinese rice wine
1 teaspoon cornstarch
¾ pound lean ground pork, chicken,
    or beef
1 tablespoon soy sauce
1 teaspoon dry sherry
1 tablespoon sesame oil
1 teaspoon salt
½ cup peeled and finely chopped
    fresh water chestnuts, or canned,
    drained
½ teaspoon grated fresh ginger
Peanut oil for frying

1. Remove the package of wonton wrappers from the refrigerator and let them come to room temperature.

2. If you are using fresh spinach, trim the stems and any blemished leaves, then plunge the spinach into a pot of rapidly boiling water and cook it for 1 to 2 minutes, until it is completely wilted. Drain. Wrap the cooked or thawed spinach in a kitchen towel and squeeze it to extract all the moisture. Finely chop the spinach.

3. In a medium bowl, stir together the sake and cornstarch. Add all the remaining ingredients except the peanut oil, and mix well.

4. Pour oil to a depth of 2 to 3 inches in a stockpot or Dutch oven, place it over medium

wontons are filled, fry them in the hot oil, not crowding the pot, until golden, 2 to 3 minutes. Remove them from the pot with a wire mesh skimmer, allowing excess oil to drain back into the pot. Place the cooked wontons on the wire rack, turn the oven off, and finish the frying. Serve immediately.

heat, and heat it to 375°F. Preheat the oven to 200°F. Place a wire rack on a baking sheet and set it in the oven. Have a damp towel, a dry towel, a small bowl of water, and a pastry brush handy on a large work surface.

5. While the oil is heating, prepare the wontons: Keeping the stack of wonton wrappers covered with the damp towel, remove 4 or 6 at a time and place them on the work surface. Place a teaspoon of the filling just off-center on each wrapper, and lightly brush water around two adjacent edges of a square wrapper and halfway around a gyoza skin. Fold the wrapper in half over the filling, pressing the edges together to form a triangle with square wrappers or a half-moon with gyoza skins. Then bring the tips around to meet and pinch together. Arrange the filled wrappers close together but not touching on a baking sheet, and cover with the dry towel. Continue filling and folding. (If you're using a 1-pound package of wonton wrappers, you'll have some left over. Seal them in plastic and store in the freezer or refrigerator.)

6. While you are filling the wrappers, monitor the temperature of the oil, and before filling the last batch, raise the heat if necessary so the oil reaches 375°F. As soon as all the

TWO STUFFED ASIAN SPECIALTIES

Because I live in a relatively small southern city, when I travel to larger metropolitan areas, I always prefer to eat in the small Asian restaurants. In Paris, I eat Vietnamese, in Atlanta I eat Cambodian, and in New York I like to go to the dim sum houses and eat wontons and spring rolls until I am stuffed. Filled dumplings can be steamed, warmed in soups, or, best yet, fried to a golden brown. I've learned to make them at home to satisfy my wanderlust. The recipes given here contain meat, but you can stuff the spring rolls and wontons with whatever you choose.

SPRING ROLLS

MAKES ABOUT 24 SPRING ROLLS

Friends who have lived in Asia tell me that the heavy egg rolls common in Chinese-American restaurants bear little resemblance to authentic spring rolls. Nancie Mc-Dermott, an expert on Thai cooking, says to look for frozen spring roll wrappers in the freezers in Asian markets. "They contain no egg and fry up crisp and golden, no bubbles," she told me.

You can fry these in a wok and save oil, but if you're not proficient with a wok, you may be more comfortable with a flat-bottomed pan. I make these rolls several hours in advance and keep them in the refrigerator before frying; the chilled rolls cook more evenly and don't burn on the bottom. I serve them with Nancie's Sweet-Hot Garlic Sauce as appetizers before all sorts of meals, and like the Vietnamese, I include lettuce leaves to hold the hot rolls.

1 tablespoon tiny dried cloud ears
   (see Note)
1 tablespoon cornstarch
½ pound bean sprouts
Peanut oil
½ cup finely chopped celery
½ cup finely chopped shallots or onions
3 cloves garlic, minced
½ pound ground pork
2 tablespoons Asian fish sauce,
   such as *nuoc mam* or *nam pla*
   (see Note, page 184)
½ teaspoon freshly ground black pepper
½ pound small raw shrimp, peeled and
   minced
1 pound (1 package) spring roll
   wrappers, thawed in the refrigerator
   if frozen

Cilantro and lettuce leaves, for garnish
Nancie's Sweet-Hot Garlic Sauce
   (page 177)

1. In a medium-size bowl, cover the mushrooms with warm water and soak for 30 minutes. Drain, saving about 2 tablespoons of the soaking liquid.

2. In a small bowl, stir together the reserved mushroom liquid and the cornstarch. Place near the stove. Trim the mushrooms of any hard parts and slice them into very thin strips. Place the strips in a bowl with the bean sprouts.

3. Heat a wok or large skillet over medium-high heat until it is hot. Carefully add 1½

tablespoons peanut oil, swirl it around to coat the surface, and then add the celery, shallots, and garlic. Stir-fry until the vegetables have softened, about 5 minutes.

4. Add the pork and stir-fry until it is no longer pink, about 2 minutes. Add the fish sauce, pepper, and shrimp, and toss well. Then add the mushrooms and bean sprouts. Stir-fry the mixture so that everything is well mixed and warmed through. Add the cornstarch mixture and mix in well. Turn off the heat and lift the contents out of the pan with a wire mesh skimmer or slotted spoon, letting the excess liquid drain off. Place on a platter to cool.

5. Meanwhile, remove the package of spring roll wrappers from the refrigerator and let them come to room temperature.

6. Open the package of spring roll wrappers and gently separate them, placing them back in a pile and covering the pile with a damp towel. Have a small bowl of water and a pastry brush handy. Line a baking sheet with wax paper or parchment and place it nearby. Place one wrapper, smooth side down, on the work surface, with one of the corners facing you. Place a heaping tablespoon of filling about one third of the way in from the point, and spread it out to form a 4-inch log. Fold the corner up and over the filling, tucking it in. Fold the right and left sides in toward the middle, and gently smooth them down. Paint the exposed flap lightly with water, then finish rolling the spring roll. Place it on the prepared baking sheet, seam side down. Continue with the remaining wrappers and filling, placing

them on the baking sheet so that they don't touch. Cover the baking sheet with plastic wrap. (You can make two layers of spring rolls, separated by plastic wrap, if you need to.) Refrigerate for 30 minutes or up to 6 hours.

7. You can pan-fry or deep-fry the rolls, but deep-frying is easier to control. To deep-fry, pour oil to a depth of 3 inches in a stockpot, wok, or Dutch oven. (To pan-fry, pour enough oil into a large skillet to come at least halfway up the sides of the rolls.) Heat the oil over medium heat to 365°F. Preheat the oven to 200°F. Place a wire rack on a baking sheet and set it in the oven.

8. Slip the rolls, one at a time, into the hot oil, carefully monitoring the temperature (do not let it go below 350°F). Do not crowd the pot. Fry the rolls until they are crispy and golden brown all over, about 4 minutes. Use tongs to gently lift the rolls, letting any excess oil drip back into the pot. Place the rolls on the wire rack to stay warm and drain further while you fry the remaining rolls. When they are all fried, pile them on a platter rimmed with cilantro and lettuce leaves, and serve with ramekins of Nancie's Sweet-Hot Garlic Sauce.

Note: These dried mushrooms, also known as tree ears, wood ears, and wood fungi, are found in Asian markets. If you can't find them, use ¼ cup coarsely chopped fresh mushrooms, sautéed until very soft.

CHAPTER 6

VEGETABLES

So vast is the variety of recipes for frying vegetables that an entire book could be written on the subject! This chapter includes southern favorites like fried baby artichokes, buttery sautés from France, three ways to fry okra, and four ways to fry potatoes. There are chips and fritters and blossoms and eggplants, beans and greens and delicate herbs and pasta. There's a salad, several appetizers, a garnish, some side dishes, and—in a world all its own—deep-fried dill pickles! In short, something for everyone.

You'll find a recipe for fried peanuts in this chapter; they are, after all, legumes, not real nuts (though you can substitute cashews or macadamia nuts for the peanuts). It's the one exception to the rule of frying at temperatures around 365°F. They're delicious snacks.

FRIED BABY ARTICHOKES

SERVES 4

I lived for a while on the Italian Riviera, where garlic, basil, and olives are grown on the rocky cliffs that plunge into the Mediterranean. In the far western corner of the region, artichokes are grown on the little coastal plain around San Remo. San Remo artichokes are considered to be the finest in Italy. Like the small purplish artichokes that are grown on other European coasts, they are not simply "baby" or immature globe artichokes, but a different variety entirely. They can be eaten raw, but they are most often fried and served as a first course.

This dish is found throughout the Mediterranean basin—in Sicily, Provence, and Liguria as well as in Spain. Elisabeth Luard is an English food writer who learned to fry in Andalusia. "That," she says, "to an artist, is like mentioning you wielded a brush in Goya's studio, or chipped a marble with Michelangelo. The frying pans of Andalusia, says the rest of Spain, turn out the food of the angels. And the cooks of Cádiz, says the rest of Andalusia, can fry the very sea spray." She recommends serving Manzanilla, the salty dry sherry of Sanlúcar, with this dish.

You're not likely to find the European cultivars in this country, but you can use baby globe artichokes for this dish. Grown in California, they appear in markets in the spring. Just make sure they are truly immature and lack the spiny choke, or they will be bitter and tough. Most Sicilian-Americans coat the artichokes with flour or batter, but I like the unadulterated version here. Be sure to use a stainless-steel knife to cut the artichokes and lemon; carbon will stain them black.

**12 baby artichokes with 2 to 3½ inches
of stem**
2 lemons
Coarse sea salt
Olive oil for frying

1. Fill a nonreactive pot (not aluminum or cast iron) with water, bring it to a rapid boil, and add the artichokes. Cook them until they have just brightened in color and give slightly to the touch, from 2 to 5 minutes depending on their size. (If you have the genuine small artichokes from Europe, no longer than 2 inches, you can eliminate this step.) Fill a large bowl with ice water and squeeze the juice from half of one of the lemons into it. Drain the artichokes and immediately plunge them into the ice water. Squeeze the juice from the second

half of the cut lemon into a bowl large enough to hold all the artichokes.

2. When the artichokes are cool enough to handle, place each one on a cutting surface and cut off the pointed end with a sharp knife. Trim off the tip of the stem, but leave the stem intact. Peel off the tough outer leaves, taking any stringy covering on the stem with them; stop peeling as soon as you have reached tender or light green leaves. Slice each artichoke in half lengthwise (through the stem too). If the artichokes are on the large side, quarter them. As you pre-pare the artichokes, place them in the bowl with the lemon juice and toss them around, sprinkling them with sea salt as you go.

3. Pour olive oil to a depth of 1 inch in a heavy skillet, and place it over medium heat. When the oil reaches 365°F, pat the artichokes dry and drop them in the skillet without crowding it. Allow them to fry in the oil until they are golden brown and crisped on the edges; they should be fork-tender but not falling apart. It will take about 2 minutes on each side. Remove the artichokes from the pan and drain them on paper towels. Quarter the remaining lemon, and serve the artichokes with the lemon alongside.

BLACK-EYED PEA CAKES

SERVES 3 AS A MAIN DISH, 6 AS APPETIZER OR SIDE DISH

These fancy—but easy—refried beans can be made with any leftover beans, such as limas, pintos, chickpeas, or black beans, as well as black-eyed peas. You can serve them as an appetizer, a side dish, or with a salad for lunch. If you don't have home-cooked peas or beans, use a 1-pound can that contains nothing but the peas or beans, water, and salt. The Go-Withs chapter has several sauces that pair well with these pan-fried cakes: the raw Salsa or the cooked Tomato Sauce, the Roasted Red Pepper Purée, the Garlic Mayonnaise or the Tartar Sauce (see Index). You can also simply splash them with hot sauce.

2 cups cooked, drained black-eyed peas
1 large egg, separated
1 teaspoon mixed dried herbs, such as
    herbes de Provence or Italian
    seasoning, or 1 tablespoon chopped
    fresh herbs of your choice
¼ cup chopped scallions (including
    some of the green tops)
1 clove garlic, minced
¼ cup chopped roasted red bell pepper
    (page 173), or ¼ cup (1 small jar)
    sliced pimientos with their juice
1 jalapeño pepper, seeded, deribbed,
    and chopped, or bottled hot sauce, to
    taste, or hot chili powder, to taste
¼ teaspoon freshly ground cumin (omit
    if you use chili powder)
Salt and freshly ground black pepper,
    to taste
¾ cup very fine dry bread crumbs
3 tablespoons peanut oil or clarified
    butter (page 8) for frying

1. Mash the peas in a medium-size mixing bowl with a large fork, a potato masher, or your hand; do not use a blender or food processor. Add the egg yolk and mix well. Then add the herbs, scallions, garlic, bell pepper, jalapeño, and cumin. Mix again and season to taste with salt and pepper. Fold in ½ cup of the bread crumbs. Put the remaining crumbs in a shallow bowl.

2. Beat the egg white until it forms soft peaks, and fold it into the mixture.

3. Form the mixture into three large burger-like patties or six smaller ones, and dust them with the bread crumbs, coating both sides well and shaking off any excess.

4. Heat the oil in a large skillet over medium-high heat. Add the patties and fry until golden all over, about 2 minutes per side. Serve immediately.

FETTUCCINE WITH CHICKPEAS

SERVES 4

Throughout Italy the legacy of centuries of trade with the Arab world is revealed in the language. The dialects of ancient port cities like Genoa and Brindisi are full of Arabic; often those words are for foodstuffs. I learned to make this regional specialty in the tiny village of Acaya, in Apulia, where it's called *ciceri e tria* (chickpeas and fettuccine). *Ciceri* is Latin for chickpea. *Tria* is Arabic; the word appears in the Genoese dialect as well.

In Apulia, the heel of the Italian boot, pasta is made—both commercially and at home—with nothing but semolina flour and water. Semolina is made from hard durum wheat, which is grown in the area. The best store-bought pasta in the world comes from Apulia; I've never tasted pasta as good. It has an earthy flavor of grain and a meaty consistency. Almost no American cookbook gives instructions for making pasta the way they do in Italy; eggs are invariably included in the dough in the American version.

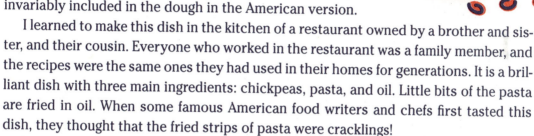

I learned to make this dish in the kitchen of a restaurant owned by a brother and sister, and their cousin. Everyone who worked in the restaurant was a family member, and the recipes were the same ones they had used in their homes for generations. It is a brilliant dish with three main ingredients: chickpeas, pasta, and oil. Little bits of the pasta are fried in oil. When some famous American food writers and chefs first tasted this dish, they thought that the fried strips of pasta were cracklings!

In Apulia, the chickpeas are slowly simmered in a clay pot while the pasta is being made. You'll have to soak them overnight, so begin the night before. Many American food writers will tell you that you can't make pasta with the semolina available in the States. That's not true, but you must use a very fine semolina flour. Serve this unusual dish as a first course.

½ **pound dried chickpeas, preferably imported from Italy**
1 **rib celery**
1 **carrot**
1 **clove garlic**
1 **medium onion stuck with 2 cloves**
3 **or 4 sprigs of parsley**
6 **peppercorns**
3 **cups fine semolina flour (see Sources, page 189)**
Salt
1 **cup warm water**
All-purpose or bread flour, for dusting

¾ **cup olive oil**
Freshly ground black pepper, to taste

1. Soak the chickpeas overnight in water to cover.

2. About 3 hours before you plan to serve them, rinse the chickpeas well and place them in a heavy saucepan with the celery, carrot, garlic, onion, parsley, and peppercorns. Add water to cover by no more than ¾ inch. Simmer the mixture, uncovered, without stirring, until the chickpeas are cooked through but still firm, 1 to 2

hours, depending on the size and age of the chickpeas. If the water level drops below the tops of the chickpeas, add a little more water, but no more than 1 cup at a time.

3. In the meantime, make the pasta dough: Place the semolina flour in a food processor and add ¼ teaspoon salt. Turn the processor on and gradually add the water, stopping the machine when the dough forms a ball.

4. Dust a work surface with the all-purpose flour and place the dough on it. Knead the dough as though it were for bread: Use the heels of your hands to push the dough away from you, then turn the dough a quarter-turn, fold it over, and continue the process until the dough is very soft but not too elastic, about 10 to 15 minutes. Wrap the dough in a plastic bag and set it aside to rest for at least 30 minutes at room temperature or for up to 6 hours refrigerated.

5. To roll the pasta, I highly recommend a pasta machine unless you have a very large marble or chopping-block counter and a long rolling pin (in Acaya, it was as long as a broom handle). Divide the dough into four portions, keeping the unused portions well covered. Set the pasta machine on its widest setting. Flatten one of the portions of dough, dust it lightly with flour, and run it through the machine. Fold the ends of the dough into the center, so that the dough is now one third its length, rotate it a quarter-turn, and run it through the machine again. Repeat the flouring, folding, and rolling until the dough is very smooth and its width is that of the machine. Continue the rolling process, decreasing the gap between the rollers a notch at a time, until the dough is about 1/16 inch thick (machines have different settings). Cut the sheet of pasta into ⅛-inch-wide fettuccine, and lay them out, not touching, on a dry towel or hang them over a broom handle balanced across the backs of two chairs to dry while you repeat the process with two more batches of the dough: With the last batch, do not set the fettuccine out to dry; cut the noodles into 1- to 2-inch pieces. Leave them on the work surface, and cover them with a damp towel.

6. When the chickpeas are done, add salt to taste. Cover the pot and cook for 10 minutes. Uncover the pot, taste for salt, correct if necessary, and remove the pot from the heat. Drain the chickpeas and remove the vegetables and peppercorns; set aside.

7. When you are ready to finish the dish, bring a large pot of water (at least 4 quarts) to a rolling boil over medium-high heat. When the water comes to a boil, add about ½ teaspoon of salt. Add the dry pasta gradually, always keeping the water at a boil. Raise the heat to high and stir the pasta occasionally so it doesn't stick to the bottom of the pot. The only way to know when the boiling pasta is done is to taste it; do so often. As soon as it loses its raw flavor, about 3 to 5 minutes, dump it out into a colander in the sink. Shake the colander to make sure all the water drains off.

8. Place the oil in a large sauté pan over medium-high heat. Uncover the 1- to 2-inch pieces of pasta and fry them in the hot oil until

FRIED ASIAN NOODLES

Italians aren't the only cooks with a seemingly limitless variety of pasta; throughout Asia, noodles and wrappers are made from wheat, rice, buckwheat, and various vegetable starches like mung bean flour. Mung bean noodles are also called threads, cellophane or transparent noodles, spring rain, harusame, saifun, fun see, or fenszu. In fact, all Asian noodles are called by dozens of names.

Many supermarkets carry several types of Asian pasta, but the best selections are in ethnic markets. They're inexpensive and last a long time, so the next time you visit an Asian market, buy several varieties and experiment.

I love Japanese soba, lumpia and pancit from the Philippines, pad Thai, and good Chinese lo mein, and I especially love them when they're deep-fried; they make an unusual garnish for any number of stewed or stir-fried dishes. Fried Asian noodles can be more than garnish, of course, but don't think of them as the starch; rice should accompany the main course as well.

Mung bean and rice noodles can be fried in deep hot oil right out of the package, or you can soak them in warm water until they become clear, drain them well, then fry them. Egg noodles must be soaked first. You will need about 2 ounces of dried noodles per person when they are accompanying the main course.

To deep-fry rice or mung bean noodles, heat oil to a depth of 3 or 4 inches in a stockpot, Dutch oven, or wok. When it reaches 375°F, fry small amounts of noodles at a time, straight from the pack for just a few seconds, until they crisp. Rice noodles will puff up and turn white almost immediately. Remove the noodles from the hot oil with a wire mesh strainer, allowing any excess oil to drain back into the pot. Place them on paper towels to drain, then use them for a garnish.

they are crispy and golden all over, about 2 minutes. Remove them with metal tongs or a wire mesh skimmer and set aside to drain on paper towels. Lower the heat under the oil to medium.

9. Add the boiled pasta and the reserved chickpeas to the oil in the skillet. Turn off the heat and toss the mixture around, making sure everything is well coated with oil. Season generously with pepper. Divide the chickpeas and pasta among four pasta bowls, garnishing each with fried pasta strips.

CORN FRITTERS

SERVES 4

These are the corn "oysters" from *The Carolina Housewife* of 1847, still one of America's best cookbooks. Though commonly served as appetizers, corn fritters make a good side dish. You can also eliminate the pepper, dust them with sugar, and serve them with fresh fruit for a delicious breakfast dish or dessert.

4 ears fresh corn, shucked
2 large eggs, separated
2 tablespoons unsalted butter, at room temperature
2 tablespoons all-purpose flour
Salt and freshly ground black pepper, to taste
¼ cup clarified butter (page 8)

1. Bring a large pot of water to a rolling boil, add the ears of corn, cover the pot, and remove from the heat. Leave the corn in the water until you are ready to use it, at least 5 minutes.

2. Using a sharp knife, cut the kernels from the cobs, so that they fall into a mixing bowl. Add the egg yolks and butter and mix well.

3. Season the flour with salt and pepper. Beat the egg whites until they hold soft peaks. Then fold the whites into the corn mixture, adding a little of the flour with each fold.

4. Heat the clarified butter in a skillet over medium-high heat. Using two tablespoons, scoop up some of the batter and form it into an oblong shape by turning it between the spoons. If you like, make three-sided oblong shapes like French *quenelles*. Lay the fritters in the hot butter and fry on all sides until golden brown, about 1½ minutes per side. Serve immediately.

EGGPLANT HOME FRIES

SERVES 6

They called this "French Fried Eggplant" at the old Berry's-on-the-Hill Restaurant in Orangeburg, South Carolina, my hometown. The vegetables and fish were always local and fresh at Berry's, which was the only Duncan Hines–recommended restaurant in the area before interstate highways were built. It was a famous stop along Highway 301, one of the old major North–South corridors.

One large eggplant will serve three people. Be sure to buy firm ones with bright green tops; they're less likely to have seeds.

2 large, very firm eggplants
Salt
Peanut oil for deep-frying
½ cup fine white cornmeal or
corn flour (see box, page 41)

1. About 45 minutes before serving, peel the eggplants and cut them into strips as for large French fries. Place them in a bowl of salted ice water and set aside for about 30 minutes.

2. Preheat the oven to 200°F. Place a wire rack on a baking sheet and set it in the oven.

3. Drain the eggplant well. Pour oil into a stockpot or Dutch oven to a depth of at least 2 inches, and heat it to 365°F over medium-high heat. Meanwhile, put the cornmeal in a shallow bowl and dust the eggplant strips well on all sides, shaking off any excess.

4. When the oil reaches 365°F, fry the eggplant in batches until golden brown, about 3 minutes. Transfer the fries to the wire rack to drain and stay warm while you finish the frying. Serve immediately.

STUFFED EGGPLANT

SERVES 4

This is a common variation of *mozzarella in carrozza* (called Mozzarella Sandwiches, in this book). Here the "carriage" (*carrozza*) is eggplant rather than bread. My friend Arnold Cerasoli is a first-generation Abruzzese-American; his family is from Capistrano. He—and nobody else that I've heard—calls the classic dip in flour, egg, and bread crumbs "febbing." It holds the sandwich together.

Arnold's daughter Celia makes these with her homemade mozzarella; she serves them in her restaurant (Celia's, in Charleston, South Carolina) on a pool of tomato sauce. They make a wonderful appetizer.

½ **pound mozzarella cheese,**
    preferably fresh
3 **medium eggplants, very firm with**
    bright green stems
Salt
1 **tablespoon chopped fresh basil**
Peanut oil for deep-frying
½ **cup all-purpose flour**
2 **large eggs**
1 **cup fine dry bread crumbs**
Tomato Sauce (page 170; see step 1)

1. About 45 minutes before serving, cut the mozzarella into ¼-inch-thick slices. Peel the eggplants and cut two ¼-inch-thick slices for each piece of mozzarella. (If you are using a commercial block of mozzarella, you can trim the eggplant to form a square shape.) Place the eggplant slices in a colander in a sink and sprinkle liberally with salt. Cover the mozzarella and place it in the refrigerator.

2. After the eggplant has drained for 30 minutes, rinse it in cold water and pat it completely dry. Preheat the oven to 200°F. Place a wire rack on a baking sheet and set it in the oven.

3. Lay half the eggplant slices out on a work surface and distribute half of the chopped basil evenly over them. Remove the mozzarella from the refrigerator and place one slice on each of the eggplant slices. Scatter the remaining basil over the mozzarella, and then top with the remaining eggplant slices to form "sandwiches."

4. Pour oil to a depth of at least 3 inches in a stockpot or Dutch oven, place it over medium-high heat, and heat it to 375°F.

5. While the oil is heating, place the flour in one shallow bowl, the eggs in another, and the bread crumbs in a third. Beat the eggs well so that no white is evident.

6. When the oil reaches 375°F, pick up a sandwich and dip it first in the flour, then in the egg, then in the bread crumbs, making sure that the entire surface of the sandwich is covered with crumbs. Use tongs to lower each sandwich into the oil; you may have to continue holding it down in the oil. Fry until golden brown all over, about 4 minutes. Transfer the sandwich to the wire rack to drain and stay warm while you bread and fry the remaining sandwiches. Serve immediately, on a pool of warm Tomato Sauce.

BITTER GREENS

SERVES 4

You might find a similar dish in Italy, with olive oil in place of the sesame oil and lemon juice instead of the rice vinegar. Italians and Chinese have long been partial to bitter greens, which are only recently becoming popular in the United States. Asian and Italian markets are good sources for all sorts of bitter greens—look for mustard greens or rape greens (also known as broccoli rabe, broccoletti di rape, or rapini); they'll all do. Serve them as a side dish to a bold-flavored main course.

You can use spinach or bok choy in this dish as well, but you won't have to wilt it first.

4 quarts water
1 pound young mustard or rape
    leaves, trimmed of tough stems
    and any yellow spots, and cut or
    torn into pieces
3 tablespoons sesame oil

2 cloves garlic, minced
¼ teaspoon hot red pepper
    flakes
Salt and freshly ground black
    pepper, to taste
1 tablespoon rice vinegar

1. In a large pot, bring the water to a full boil. Plunge the greens into the water and allow to cook for 2 to 3 minutes, or until all the leaves are completely wilted. Lift the greens from the water with tongs or a wire mesh strainer, and place in a colander to drain. Turn off the heat and set the cooking water aside.

2. In a large sauté pan that has a lid, heat the sesame oil over medium-high heat until it is very hot. Add the garlic and toss it around for about 10 seconds. Do not let it brown. Add the pepper flakes and the wilted greens and toss continuously until the greens are evenly heated. Remove from the heat and taste. If they aren't done to your liking, cover the pan, lower the heat to a simmer, and cook for 5 minutes. If there is not enough liquid clinging to the leaves, add up to ¼ cup of the reserved cooking water.

3. Season with salt and pepper. Serve either hot or at room temperature, splashing the rice vinegar onto the greens just before serving.

FRIED OKRA SALAD WITH FRESH CORN AND TOMATOES

SERVES 6

All over the country, chefs are brightening traditional summer vegetable dishes with their inspired variations. This one is a combination of ideas from Birmingham's Chris Hastings and Dallas's Stephan Pyles, both of them thoroughly modern and southern to the bone. Be sure to make it at summer's height, when the okra, corn, and tomatoes are garden-fresh and full of flavor.

6 perfectly ripe slicing tomatoes

1½ pounds very small fresh okra pods (about 30)

¼ cup buttermilk

3 large ears fresh sweet corn, such as Silver Queen, shucked

3 scallions (including the green tops), thinly sliced

3 tablespoons fresh lemon juice

¼ cup olive oil

¼ cup extra-virgin olive oil

Salt and freshly ground black pepper, to taste

½ cup cornmeal

½ cup corn flour (see box, page 41) or all-purpose flour

Peanut oil for frying

1. Wash and core the tomatoes, and set them aside at room temperature. Trim the okra of stems, and place the pods in a small bowl with the buttermilk. Toss every so often to keep them coated.

2. Drop the corn into a pot of boiling salted water, and remove as soon as it is tender, about 1 minute.

3. Place the scallions in a medium-size bowl, and add the lemon juice. Make a dressing by whisking in both olive oils. Season with

salt and pepper, to taste. Cut the kernels from the corncobs into the dressing, then stir to mix well.

4. Combine the cornmeal and corn flour in a medium-size bowl. Season heavily with salt and pepper, and toss well.

5. Pour oil into a stockpot or Dutch oven, to a depth of at least 2 inches, and heat it to 365°F over medium heat.

FRIED OKRA

I don't know why some people don't like okra, though I notice that it falls into the category of foods that they say they'll eat "if it's fried." I *love* okra, but it is the vegetable that I am pickiest about. I try to get to the local farmer's market as soon as it opens in the summer so that I can choose bright green okra pods, all finger-length, with no dark signs whatsoever. They should be firm but with no spines. They should give to the touch and smell faintly of the salt marsh. If you can't find just-picked okra where you live, buy it frozen: it is vastly superior to old, blackened okra pods several days out of the field.

Here you'll find several recipes for fried okra: traditional corn flour–dusted okra, tempura fritters, and buttermilk-soaked okra fried as a garnish for a tomato salad.

6. While the oil is heating, slice the tomatoes, season them with salt and pepper, and divide them among six serving plates. Using a slotted spoon, scatter the corn dressing over the tomatoes.

7. Drain the okra, and toss it in the cornmeal mix, shaking off the excess. When the oil reaches 365°F, fry the okra until golden brown, about 3 minutes, working in batches if necessary. Remove the okra from the oil with a wire mesh strainer, allowing any excess oil to drain back into the pot. Place the okra on paper towels to drain further while you fry the rest.

8. Add a pile of fried okra to each plate, and serve immediately.

TRADITIONAL FRIED OKRA

SERVES 4

This is the preparation you'll find throughout the South and Southwest. Corn flour is a very fine grind of cornmeal. If you can't find it, pulse some cornmeal in a blender to get a finer grind.

1 pound fresh okra
Peanut oil for deep-frying
1 cup corn flour (see box, page 41)
Salt and freshly ground black pepper,
    to taste
Cayenne pepper, to taste

1. About 30 minutes before you plan to fry the okra, trim the stem ends from the pods and slice the pods into ½-inch pieces. Place them in a bowl of ice water.

2. Pour oil to a depth of 2 to 3 inches in a stockpot or Dutch oven, place it over medium-high heat, and heat it to 370°F.

3. While the oil is heating, drain the okra well. In a shallow flat bowl, combine the corn flour with the salt, black pepper, and cayenne. Line a colander with crumpled paper towels.

4. When the oil reaches 370°F, dust the okra well with the corn flour, and fry it in the hot oil until golden, about 3 minutes. Maintain the temperature and don't crowd the pot. Remove the okra with a wire mesh skimmer and drain it in the prepared colander before serving.

OKRA FRITTERS

SERVES 4

These tempura fritters call for perfect okra pods, fastidiously trimmed. Cut the stem end down to, but not into, the pod. If fresh okra is not available, use frozen whole pods.

1 pound small fresh okra pods,
    trimmed (see headnote), or
    1 package (10 ounces) frozen
    whole okra, thawed
Peanut oil for deep-frying
Salt and freshly ground black pepper,
    to taste
1 large egg yolk
1 cup ice water
1 cup all-purpose flour
Salt, for serving

1. If you are using fresh okra, place the trimmed okra in a saucepan that has a tight-fitting lid and add just enough water to cover the bottom of the pot (about ⅓ cup). Cover tightly and steam over medium-high heat for about 5 minutes, or until the water evaporates. Transfer the okra to a kitchen towel; pat it dry and allow it to cool. If you are using frozen okra, place it on the towel after it has thawed, and pat it dry.

2. Pour oil to a depth of 2 inches in a deep skillet or stockpot, place it over medium-high heat, and heat it to 365°F. Place a wire rack on a baking sheet.

3. While the oil is heating, season the okra with salt and pepper. In a wide bowl, thoroughly mix the egg yolk and ice water with a wooden spoon. Dump the flour into the liquid all at once, stirring quickly. The batter will be lumpy.

4. When the oil reaches 365°F, hold an okra pod by the stem end, drag it through the batter to coat completely, and drop it into the hot oil. Continue, frying each pod for 1 to 2 minutes, until they just start to brown. As they are cooked, transfer the okra pods to the wire rack to drain. Do not crowd the pot, and keep the oil at 365°F.

5. Let everyone salt the okra to taste. (If you salt it before it is served, it will become soggy.) Be careful—these are hot!

ONION RINGS

SERVES 8

If you dip onion rings in milk and flour, they'll fry to a golden brown with a crispy coating, but I prefer this thick beer batter. Not only does it remind me of the onion rings from the drive-in restaurants of my youth, it also covers the sweet onion flesh so it doesn't cook too much. I like to fry these outside over a camp stove. I serve my guests drinks on the patio, and offer them baskets of onion rings as they come out of the fryer.

Start making the batter at least an hour (but no more than 2 hours) before you plan to fry, because it must rest.

2 cups all-purpose flour
¾ teaspoon salt
1 can (12 ounces) beer, flat and at room temperature
2 tablespoons peanut oil
4 large onions (about ¾ pound each), as flat in shape as possible
Peanut oil for deep-frying
2 large egg whites
Salt, for serving

1. In a large mixing bowl, combine the flour and salt. In another bowl, combine the beer and 2 tablespoons oil. Pour the liquid into the dry ingredients, stirring with a wire whisk only until combined. Do not beat the batter. Let it stand for 1 to 2 hours.

2. Cut the onions into ½-inch-thick slices, carefully separate them into rings. (Large flat onions will separate into nice rings almost all the way to the center. Save the centers to use in a salad or another dish.)

3. Pour oil into a large pot to a depth of at least 2 inches, and heat it to 365°F over medium-high heat.

4. While the oil is heating, beat the egg whites until they hold stiff peaks. Fold them into the batter, working lightly. Place a wire rack on a baking sheet.

5. When the oil reaches 365°F, dip the onion rings into the batter to coat completely and then drop them into the oil. Do not crowd the pot. Fry until they are golden brown all over, 2 to 3 minutes on each side. Remove the onion rings from the pot, holding each ring over the pot for a moment so that any excess oil drains off. Place them on the wire rack. Continue frying until you have a plateful, then serve those immediately. They stay hot for a while. Let your diners salt their own onion rings (they'll get soggy if you salt them before serving).

6. Although it may be hard to wait for the oil to return to 365°F before adding the next batch, be sure you do, and also be sure you maintain that temperature throughout frying.

FRIED PARSLEY

Crispy unadorned fried parsley leaves are a wonderful garnish for many of the foods in this book, but you must be absolutely fastidious in their preparation or you'll end up with grease all over your kitchen. If you grow your own parsley in pots and you aren't worried about the air quality, you won't have to wash the leaves. If you must wash the leaves, though, you must also get them perfectly dry. Use a salad spinner if you have one, then place them on a terry-cloth towel and pat them thoroughly dry.

I like to fry parsley just about any time I'm having a deep-fried dish as the main course. The green color and flavor remain after the frying. After you've fried whatever else it is you're frying, make sure the oil temperature is at 365°F, then toss a small handful of clean dry leaves or sprigs into the oil, standing away from the pot. Fry them for about 20 seconds and then remove them with a wire mesh skimmer. You can drain the parsley on paper towels to make sure it isn't holding any oil; most of the oil will easily roll off the flat-leaf variety.

FRIED PEANUTS

SERVES 4

This recipe is the one exception to the rule: The nuts are begun in *cold* oil so that they cook evenly, and the oil is then heated to a mere 300°F—cool by most frying standards. You can also use cashews or macadamias in this recipe just as well. Salting the nuts is optional, but salted nuts are a wonderful accompaniment for beer. It's okay to use the peanuts with the papery red coverings; some will lose the covering and you'll be able to judge the nut color by a nude one.

½ **pound (about 1½ cups)**
shelled raw peanuts
About 1½ cups peanut oil
1 teaspoon salt or seasoned
salt (optional)

1. Place a sieve over an empty saucepan, and line a mixing bowl with paper towels.

2. Put the peanuts in a wok or a small saucepan, and cover with peanut oil. Place the pan over medium-high heat and stir the nuts with a thermometer until the oil reaches 300°F. Immediately reduce the heat to medium, and begin stirring the nuts gently and continually with a mesh scoop or slotted spoon, occasionally lifting them out of the oil to closely observe their color. Don't let the temperature of the oil go over 300°F.

3. The moment the nuts have turned golden, pour the nuts and oil into the prepared sieve. Shake the sieve a little to help the nuts drain. When they are well drained, dump them into the paper-towel-lined bowl.

4. When the nuts have cooled a little more, pull out the paper towels, patting the nuts dry. Sprinkle with the salt, if desired, and serve at room temperature. They can be stored in a plastic bag, in which they can also be frozen.

FRIED DILL PICKLES

SERVES 16

first had these odd creatures at a fried fish house on the Ogeechee River outside Savannah, Georgia. I love to serve them as appetizers to "gourmets," who usually look down their noses at such things. I've yet to meet a soul who didn't love them. This is fun party food to serve with drinks before dinner. I figure on 1½ pickles per person. The batter will coat about two dozen pickles.

3 cups all-purpose flour
½ teaspoon salt
Cayenne pepper, to taste (optional)
2 large eggs, separated
1 cup beer, flat and at room temperature
24 whole large dill pickles
Peanut oil for deep-frying

1. About 1½ hours before serving, combine 2 cups of the flour with the salt and cayenne in a large bowl. In a small bowl, mix the egg yolks with the beer. Make a well in the center of the flour and pour the beer mixture in, stirring with a wire whisk only until combined. Do not beat the batter. Let it stand for 1 hour.

2. When you are ready to fry them, slice the pickles in half lengthwise and pat them dry. Pour oil into a Dutch oven or stockpot to a depth of 3 inches, place it over medium-high heat, and heat it to 365°F. Place a wire rack on a baking sheet.

3. While the oil is heating, beat the egg whites until they hold soft peaks, and fold them gently but thoroughly into the batter. Place the remaining 1 cup flour in a small mixing bowl.

4. When the oil reaches 365°F, dust the pickle halves with the flour, making sure they are well coated. Shake off any excess. Drop them, several at a time, into the batter. Using tongs, pick up the pickles and carefully lower them into the hot oil. Fry until they are golden brown all over, 2 to 3 minutes on each side, and then transfer them to the wire rack to drain.

5. Have someone place the pickles on a serving dish or in a napkin-lined basket and pass them with cocktail napkins while you fry the next batch.

FRENCH FRIES

SERVES 6

When I lived in Paris, there was a café—not a bistro, not a brasserie, not a restaurant—that served the best *pommes frites* I've ever eaten. It was a neighborhood hangout, full of working-class men, gallery owners, students, and an occasional tourist. I remember it as always being open, though I often arrived too late for the roast chicken, the house specialty, which was always simply prepared with the finest *poulet de Bresse*. The chicken, like the steak, was served with fries.

The café was run by a husband-and-wife team; they both cooked and worked in the front of the house. Though I never knew her name, "Madame" let me in her kitchen to watch her fry potatoes. Like the English, Madame used rendered beef fat for frying. The last time I saw her, they had stopped frying altogether and had simplified their menu to mostly sandwiches. One of the art dealers in the neighborhood had hopes of maintaining the café after Madame and Monsieur retired, but I'm afraid I'll never have fries like those again.

Nevertheless, these are pretty close. I use lard, but you can use peanut oil as well. The potatoes are fried twice, once at a lower temperature, then quickly again in hotter fat. Beef fat or lard will begin to smoke if it goes above 375°F; you must put the fries in the second it reaches that temperature. Madame fried all of her potatoes for the day ahead of time, then set her fryer at the higher temperature and flash-fried them to order. Her fryer had a basket that allowed excess oil to drain off; she did not pat them dry, but simply dumped them out onto the plates and served them piping hot.

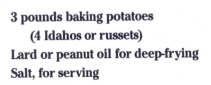

**3 pounds baking potatoes
(4 Idahos or russets)
Lard or peanut oil for deep-frying
Salt, for serving**

1. At least 30 minutes and up to 2 hours before serving, peel the potatoes and cut them into ¼-inch-thick matchsticks. Lay the potatoes out on a towel and fold it up around

them so that they don't darken while you heat the lard. Line a large colander with crumpled paper towels, and set it aside.

2. Put lard or oil in a deep pot to a depth of 3 inches. Heat it over medium heat to 350°F. Fry the potatoes in five or six batches, about 1 cup at a time. As each batch is lightly browned, about 7 minutes, remove all of the potatoes from the oil with a wire mesh strainer, allowing any excess oil to drain back into the pot before placing them in the colander. Place more crumpled paper towels on top of the batch before adding the next. Fry all of the potatoes. Then transfer them from the colander to a baking sheet, discarding the paper towels and patting the potatoes dry of all grease. Place them in a dry place, such as an unheated oven. Remove the pot from the heat until you are ready to finish frying.

3. When you are ready, reheat the fat to 375°F. Be very careful if you are using lard—do not let it get any hotter. Place a wire rack on another baking sheet. Fry the potatoes in batches again, keeping the oil right at 375°F,

POTATOES

In France, French fries (*pommes frites*) aren't the only fried potatoes: there are also straw potatoes, matchsticks, Pont Neuf potatoes, waffled potatoes, souffléed potatoes, birds' nests, and various potato croquettes and fritters. I've included four recipes for frying potatoes: two for precooked potatoes, one for potato chips (page 136), and one for my perfect French fries. Follow the instructions to a tee and you won't be disappointed.

until they are golden brown, 1 to 2 minutes. Transfer them immediately to the wire rack to drain, and finish the frying. Do not salt the French fries until you serve them; better yet, let each diner salt his or her own so they don't get soggy.

PAN-FRIED POTATOES

SERVES 4

If you boil potatoes before you pan-fry them, the insides will be light and fluffy and the outsides will be crunchy and brown. You'll need about 30 minutes to prepare them, so plan accordingly. Serve these hot with steaks, chops, and roasts.

2 pounds potatoes (about 12 new
potatoes, 6 white potatoes, or
2 or 3 Idahos), unpeeled
¼ cup olive oil
1 teaspoon salt
Freshly ground black pepper, to taste
1 tablespoon minced fresh herbs of
your choice
2 or 3 garlic cloves, minced

1. Cut small new potatoes in half or larger potatoes into 1½-inch wedges. Cook them in a large pot of boiling water until they are partially cooked but are still firm and hold their shape, about 10 minutes depending on the type of potato. Drain the potatoes and allow them to dry.

2. Heat the oil in a large heavy frying pan over medium-high heat. When it is hot, add the potatoes. They should form a single layer that covers the bottom of the pan. Sprinkle ½ teaspoon of the salt and the pepper over the potatoes, and allow them to fry in the oil without stirring for about 10 minutes or until they are golden brown on the bottom.

3. Shake the pan gently to loosen the potatoes, then turn them with tongs or a metal spatula. If they are browned but are still sticking to the pan, scrape them off the bottom of the pan by pushing firmly with the spatula turned upside down. Make sure all of the potatoes are turned over. Sprinkle the remaining ½ teaspoon salt over the potatoes and fry until they are well browned all over, turning the wedges if necessary. It will take about 10 minutes more. About 30 seconds before removing the potatoes from the pan, sprinkle them with the minced herbs and the garlic, and shake the pan to evenly distribute the seasonings.

4. Lift the potatoes from the pan with a slotted spatula, allowing the oil to drain off into the pan. Serve immediately.

ITALIAN POTATO FRITTERS

MAKES 16

Apulia, the southeastern tip of Italy, is the breadbasket of the country. The heel of the boot, the Salentine peninsula is known for its seemingly endless groves of olive trees, wheat fields, artichokes, and greens. The food is the healthy Mediterranean diet composed mostly of olive oil, pasta, beans, and green vegetables. Salentine antipasti, not likely to include meats, feature several dishes of fritters followed by *carciofi sott'olio* (marinated artichokes) and plate after plate of wilted greens, both wild and cultivated varieties of chicory, mustard, and turnip.

I learned to make these potato fritters in Acaya, the only remaining fortified city in the area. They were one of six or seven different fritters served as a matter of course in the family-run restaurant in this town of 450 families. One of the family members called these croquettes, but throughout the region they are known as *panzarotti*.

The dense and fresh ricotta that is made in Italy from the whey of mozzarella—both freshly made each morning—is all but impossible to find in the States. These fritters will taste just fine if you use the best American-made ricotta you can find. Look for an all-natural brand, made from whole milk; its texture will be closer to the Italian.

Olive oil for frying
1 pound potatoes, boiled and peeled
¼ pound ricotta cheese
2 large eggs, lightly beaten
1 tablespoon chopped fresh mint leaves
Salt and freshly ground black pepper,
    to taste
1 cup fine dry bread crumbs

1. Pour oil to a depth of about 1 inch in a large heavy skillet or sauté pan, and place it over medium-high heat. Place a wire rack on a baking sheet and set it aside.

2. Mash the potatoes in a large mixing bowl, or run them through a ricer or food mill into the bowl. Add the ricotta, eggs, mint, and salt and pepper. Mix well.

3. Place the bread crumbs in a shallow bowl. Just as the surface of the oil begins to ripple, but before it smokes, moisten your hands and form little fritters of the potato mixture, about the width of two fingers and the length of one. Roll the fritters in the bread crumbs and fry them in the hot oil until golden brown all over, about a minute or so on each side. Transfer the fritters to the wire rack, and blot dry with paper towels if necessary before serving.

FRIED SQUASH BLOSSOMS

SERVES 6 TO 8

Here's a recipe that's found around the Mediterranean, in Southeast Asia, and in the American South and Southwest. These fried blossoms make a quick and delightful summer appetizer. If the blossoms come from unsprayed plants and are picked early in the morning, you should not have to wash them. The blossoms of other squash, pumpkin, and melon plants—as well as sliced vegetables and shrimp—can be used in this tempura batter. Blossoms can also be stuffed before frying. Be sure to try the recipe for them (facing page) as well.

Peanut oil for frying
24 squash blossoms with 2-inch stems
1 large egg yolk
1 cup ice water
1 cup all-purpose flour
Salt, to taste

1. Pour oil to a depth of 2 inches in a large deep skillet or Dutch oven, place it over medium-high heat, and heat it to 365°F. Preheat the oven to 200°F. Place a wire rack on a baking sheet and set it in the oven.

2. While the oil is heating, check the blossoms for bugs and sand. Wash and pat dry if necessary. In a wide bowl, mix the egg yolk well with the ice water, using a wooden spoon. Pour the flour into the liquid all at once, stirring quickly. The batter will be lumpy.

3. When the oil reaches 365°F, start to fry the blossoms. Holding each blossom by the stem, drag it through the batter and drop it into the hot oil. Fry the blossoms for about 30 seconds on one side, then flip them over and fry until they have begun to brown, 10 to 20 seconds. Remove each blossom as it is cooked and place it on the wire rack in the oven. Continue until all the blossoms are fried. Salt lightly, and serve immediately.

STUFFED SQUASH BLOSSOM TEMPURA

SERVES 4

This recipe came to me from Mark Miller and Leland Atkinson at Washington, D.C.'s popular Red Sage; it's typical of the restaurant's Southwest-inspired fare. Squash blossoms have been stuffed and fried forever, but two clever touches highlight this dish as theirs: the masa harina (for flavor) and the club soda (for lightness).

This is fairly elaborate restaurant cooking, but it's not complicated. You'll need to do a few things in advance, like toasting the pumpkin seeds, roasting the garlic, and making the guajillo purée. It's worth it. You can substitute finely ground corn flour for the masa harina if you like. It won't taste exactly the same, but it is just as delicious.

Manchego is a Spanish cheese made from sheep's milk. If you can find it, buy the hard form for grating; if you can't, use Parmesan. The cheese and mushrooms invite a smoky tomato sauce. Try the Grilled Tomato Hot Sauce (see Index) with the squash blossoms.

FOR THE STUFFING
4 medium portobello mushrooms, stems removed
2 tablespoons olive oil
2 teaspoons salt
1½ teaspoons freshly ground black pepper
2 teaspoons chopped fresh sage leaves
¼ cup freshly grated Manchego or Parmesan cheese
2 tablespoons chopped fresh chives
2 teaspoons roasted garlic purée (see Notes)
2 tablespoons toasted pumpkin seeds (see Notes)
2 teaspoons guajillo purée (see Notes)

FOR THE BLOSSOMS AND BATTER
16 squash blossoms
Corn or peanut oil for frying
2½ cups club soda or sparkling water, chilled
2 large eggs
1 cup masa harina (see Sources, page 189) or corn flour (see box, page 41)
½ cup all-purpose flour

1. Preheat the broiler or prepare a hot fire in a grill.

2. Scrape the black ribs from the underside of the mushroom caps, if desired. Combine the oil, salt, and pepper in a bowl and mix well. Toss the mushrooms in the oil, coating them well. Then grill or broil the mushrooms about 4 inches from the heat source until they just become limp, 3 to 6 minutes.

3. Dice the mushrooms. Then purée half of them in a food processor or blender. Just before stuffing the blossoms, toss the puréed and diced mushrooms with the remaining stuffing ingredients and correct the seasoning to suit your palate.

4. Prepare the squash blossoms: Trim the stems of the blossoms if desired, but leave a ½- to 1-inch piece to use as a handle. Carefully peel back the petals, and fill the cavity with just enough filling to make a snug parcel. Fold the petals back around the filling, overlapping and sealing them as well as possible. Fill all of the blossoms, placing them on a baking sheet as they are done. Place the filled blossoms in the refrigerator to chill, uncovered, for at least 30 minutes or up to 6 hours before cooking.

5. When you are ready to fry the squash blossoms, pour oil to a depth of 2 inches in a large deep skillet or Dutch oven. Place it over medium heat, and heat to 350°F.

6. While the oil is heating, preheat the oven to 200°F. Place a wire rack on a baking sheet and set it in the oven. Remove the chilled stuffed blossoms from the refrigerator.

7. Make the tempura batter: Pour the club soda into a large shallow bowl and add the eggs. Beat well. Pour in the masa harina and the flour and stir with a fork, chopsticks, or a heavy whisk until just blended. Do not overmix; lumps won't matter.

8. When the oil reaches 350°F, pick up a blossom by the stem and drag it through the batter, then over the edge of the bowl to scrape off any excess. Place it immediately in the hot oil and fry until golden brown, about 2 minutes on each side. Repeat this with the remaining blossoms. As they are cooked, transfer the blossoms to the wire rack to drain and stay warm. Serve immediately.

Notes: To roast garlic, simply place an unpeeled whole bulb in a baking pan in a 350°F oven and bake it until it gives to the touch, about 30 minutes. Squeeze out the "purée" from each clove.

You can toast the pumpkin seeds in the oven at the same time you are roasting the garlic. Place them on a baking sheet in a single layer. Roast the seeds until they are lightly colored, 10 to 15 minutes. (They can also be toasted in a dry skillet over medium heat. Shake the skillet so that they don't burn and remove them when they've stopped popping, about 5 minutes.)

Guajillo is a very common, long red dried pepper from Mexico. To make the purée, first seed and stem the pepper, then roast it in a dry skillet for about 4 minutes. Pour warm water over the pepper in the skillet just to cover, and allow it to soak, off the heat, until soft, about 20 minutes. Purée the soaked pepper in a blender, adding some of the soaking water if it isn't bitter. (If it is, use plain water.)

SWEET POTATO FRITTERS

Y ou can make this variation on hushpuppies to serve as a side dish. They can be deep- or pan-fried. If you can't find good sweet potatoes, use a winter squash and call them "squashpuppies."

Peanut oil for frying
½ cup mashed cooked sweet potatoes or
winter squash (about ½ pound raw)
2 large eggs
¼ cup cornmeal
¼ cup all-purpose flour
¼ teaspoon salt
¼ teaspoon ground cinnamon
Cayenne pepper, to taste
Freshly ground black pepper,
to taste
2 tablespoons minced onion
(optional)

1. In a stockpot, Dutch oven, or deep skillet over medium heat, begin heating the oil to 375°F. To deep-fry, you will need about 3 inches of oil. To pan-fry, you will need only ¾ inch. Place a wire rack on a baking sheet and set it aside.

2. Thoroughly mix the remaining ingredients in a large bowl. Drop the mixture by tablespoonfuls into the hot oil. In deep fat, the fritters should take about 2 minutes. In a shallow pan, you may have to cook them a little longer and turn them so that each side is browned. The exterior should be crisp and the inside moist and mousse-like. Maintain the oil temperature while you fry the fritters; as they are done, remove them to the wire rack to drain. Serve hot.

FRIED TOFU WITH DIPPING SAUCE

SERVES 4 AS AN APPETIZER

This version of *age-dashi tofu* is adapted from a recipe that came by way of Lucy Seligman, who writes a culinary newsletter, *Gochiso-sama!,* about Japan. Lucy says that the Japanese, who are among the world's best fryers, used sesame oil for frying until it became prohibitively expensive. Adding a little sesame to the vegetable oil infuses the tofu with its delicious nutty flavor. Use chopsticks to cut the tofu: the sauce will penetrate the rough-cut surfaces more thoroughly.

Kuzu is a fine white powder that is ground from the root of the kudzu vine. It is available in Japanese markets and natural-foods stores. If you can't find it, use ground arrowroot or cornstarch.

Lucy's dipping sauce is the classic Tempura Dipping Sauce, with some grated daikon and chopped scallions added. Daikon is a large elongated radish, usually white. It is widely available in supermarkets today, sometimes labeled "Japanese radish."

**2 blocks cotton (*momen*) tofu
(soft tofu)**
Tempura Dipping Sauce (page 179)
**¼ to ½ cup kuzu, arrowroot, or
cornstarch**
3 tablespoons vegetable oil
1 tablespoon sesame oil
**½ cup freshly grated daikon,
drained**
½ cup finely chopped scallions

1. Place the tofu between two plates, and set a weight, such as a large can of tomatoes, on top. Set aside for 1 hour, occasionally draining off the excess liquid.

2. Place the dipping sauce in a small saucepan and warm it over low heat while you fry the tofu. Place a double layer of paper towels near the stove. Place the kuzu in a shallow bowl.

3. Pat the tofu dry and cut it into eight equal cubes. Dust the cubes well with the kuzu.

4. Pour the vegetable and sesame oils into a heavy skillet and place it over medium-high heat. When the oil is very hot but not smoking, gently place the cubes of tofu in the skillet and cook until golden brown on all sides, 1 to 2 minutes per side. Remove and drain on the paper towels.

5. To serve, place two pieces of tofu in each serving dish (pasta bowls are perfect), and pour the warm dipping sauce over it. Top with the daikon and scallions, and serve immediately.

STIR-FRIED VEGETABLES

SERVES 4

This is the simplest way I know to cook a bunch of vegetables, especially for a crowd. Its only drawback is that it's a last-minute thing. It helps to have the vegetables chopped in advance—be sure to chop everything into equal sizes. Put the chopped veggies in self-seal plastic bags in the refrigerator until it's time to cook.

You can stir-fry just about any firm vegetable, although you may have to parboil some of the root vegetables first. Most stir-fried dishes are cooked very quickly over high heat so that the vegetables retain their shape and color. A liquid is added, the heat is lowered, and the dish is allowed to steam for a few minutes.

This stir-fry is scented with garlic and ginger. They are sautéed in the oil for just a few seconds, then removed. If you want the flavor of sesame or olive oil, add a little near the end of the steaming time.

3 tablespoons mild oil, such as peanut oil
2 cloves garlic, unpeeled
1 slice fresh ginger, about ¼ inch thick
    and 4 inches long
1 cup snow peas, trimmed
1 cup sliced shiitake mushroom caps
1 red bell pepper, cored, seeded, and
    sliced

1 cup cauliflower florets
1 cup broccoli florets
1 tablespoon soy sauce
¼ cup homemade chicken stock or
    low-sodium canned broth,
    or water
1 teaspoon sesame oil or chile
    sesame oil (optional)

1. Place a wok over high heat. Add the oil, pouring it in a circle around the rim so that it coats all of the inside surface. Swirl it around to be sure the wok is coated, using a large dry cloth to hold the handle of the wok. When the oil is very hot but not smoking, add the garlic and ginger and cook until the papery skin of the garlic begins to brown, about 20 seconds. Remove the garlic and ginger from the wok and discard.

2. Immediately add the snow peas and mushrooms all at once, tossing them around in the wok with a large metal spatula. Cook, tossing, for about 1 minute. Then add the pepper. Stir-fry for 1 minute more, then add the cauliflower. Stir-fry for 1 minute, then add the broccoli. Stir-fry for 1 minute more.

3. Add the soy sauce and the stock and bring to a boil. Immediately reduce the heat to medium-low, cover the wok, and allow the vegetables to steam for about 3 minutes, or until they are tender. After 2 minutes of steaming, add the sesame oil, if desired. Serve immediately.

TEMPURA VEGETABLES

SERVES 8

Anyone who has eaten perfectly fried tempura in a Japanese restaurant knows how delicate fried foods can be. Use whatever vegetables you want, but be sure to cut them all into small even pieces so that they cook evenly. Snow peas, mushrooms, eggplant, asparagus, and sweet potatoes are traditional ingredients in Japan, but you can use carrots, bell peppers, string beans, cauliflower, and onion rings, too. This tempura batter also works well with whitefish or with fresh shrimp.

Tempura Dipping Sauce
  (page 179)
1 eggplant (about ½ pound)
½ pound fresh small mushrooms,
    such as the common cultivated
    variety, shiitakes, or oysters
16 fresh snow peas, stemmed
1 small sweet potato, peeled and
    cut into ¼-inch-thick slices
1 green or red bell pepper, cored,
    seeded, and cut into 8 slices
Peanut oil for deep-frying
1 egg yolk
2 cups ice-cold water
⅛ teaspoon baking soda
1⅔ cups all-purpose flour

1. Divide the dipping sauce among eight ramekins and set them aside. Preheat the oven to 200°F, and place eight salad plates in it to warm. Place a wire rack on a baking sheet, and set it aside.

2. Using a vegetable peeler, peel the eggplant lengthwise, leaving several narrow strips of unpeeled skin. Halve the eggplant lengthwise, then cut it into ¼-inch-thick slices. Rinse the slices thoroughly, pat them dry, and place them at one end of a large platter.

3. Cut the mushrooms into pieces according to their size: in half for button mushrooms, into as many as 16 pieces for larger shiitakes. Place them on the platter, and add the rest of the prepared vegetables to the platter.

4. Pour oil into a stockpot or Dutch oven to a depth of 3 inches, place it over medium-high heat, and heat it to 375°F.

5. While the oil is heating, prepare the batter: In a large mixing bowl, combine the egg yolk and cold water and mix well. Stir in the baking soda. Then sift in the flour and stir with a wooden spoon.

6. Using large chopsticks or tongs, dip the vegetables into the batter one at a time, moving each piece around to be sure it is well coated. Maintaining the oil at 375°F, fry the vegetables one serving at a time: 2 pieces of eggplant, 2 snow peas, 2 mushroom halves, 1 slice of sweet potato, and 1 slice of bell pepper, flipping them after 1 minute. Fry on the second side for another minute, or until lightly golden. Remove the pieces with a wire mesh strainer and place them on the wire rack to drain. Strain any bits of batter or vegetables from the oil, and repeat the process with the second serving. When all 8 pieces are in the oil, transfer the first batch from the rack to a warmed plate in the oven. Repeat with the remaining servings, always monitoring the temperature of the oil and straining any bits of batter from the oil after each use.

7. Place a ramekin of dipping sauce on each plate of tempura vegetables, and serve immediately.

VEGETABLE CHIPS

SERVES 4

To make paper-thin chips to be deep-fried, you'll need a mandoline, the ingenious manual slicing tool from France, or a food processor fitted with the thin slicing blade. Potatoes aren't the only root vegetables that take well to deep-frying. You can use taro root, beets, celeriac, sweet potatoes, and parsnips as well. Fry these before a party, keep them in a warm oven, and serve them with drinks.

The frying of chips is easier to control at lower than normal temperatures—I recommend 350°F for this recipe. Four pounds of raw vegetables will serve about four people—you won't believe how many of these people will eat!

1 or 2 beets (about ½ pound)
1 baking potato (about 1 pound)
1 sweet potato (about 1 pound)
1 large parsnip (about ½ pound)
1 celeriac (about 1 pound)
Juice of 1 lemon
Peanut oil for frying
Salt, for serving

1. Use a mandoline or the thin slicing blade in a food processor to slice paper-thin chips of the vegetables, as follows: Peel the beets before slicing, then place the slices in a bowl of cold water. Peel the baking potato before slicing, and place the slices in another bowl of cold water. Peel the sweet potato, parsnip, and celeriac before slicing, and place the slices in a third bowl of cold water to which you then add the lemon juice (to keep the vegetables from darkening).

2. Preheat the oven to 200°F. Line a large roasting pan with paper towels and place it in the oven.

3. Pour oil into a stockpot or Dutch oven to a depth of 3 to 4 inches, place it over medium heat, and heat it to 350°F.

4. While the oil is heating, drain the beets and place them on paper (or cloth) towels; pat the beets as dry as possible. Drain the baking potatoes and place them on paper (or cloth) towels; pat them perfectly dry as well.

5. When the oil reaches 350°F, fry the beets until they are crisp with golden edges, about 2 minutes. Fry in batches, not crowding the pot, swishing them around with a wire mesh skimmer to separate them. Transfer the chips to the prepared roasting pan and place a layer of paper towels on top of the chips. When all the beets are done, fry the baking potatoes until they are crisp and brown, about 2 minutes, transferring them to the roasting pan and covering them with another layer of paper towels. While the potatoes are frying, drain the bowl of sweet potatoes, parsnips, and celeriac slices, place them on paper (or cloth) towels, and pat as dry as possible. Fry the mixed chips as for the others, about 2 minutes. Remove the roasting pan from the oven, add the chips, and place another layer of paper towels on top. Gently pat to remove any excess oil.

6. Gently remove all the layers of paper towels from the roasting pan, letting the vegetable chips fall back into the pan. Serve the chips immediately, return them to the oven to stay warm for up to an hour before serving, or let them cool to room temperature and then store them in an airtight container for up to 3 days. Do not salt until serving or the chips will become soggy.

ZUCCHINI PANCAKES

SERVES 4 TO 8

Serve these airy Italian fritters as both bread and vegetable alongside meat or rice dishes. They're very easy to make. Grate the zucchini on the large holes of a hand grater. A bit of cross-cultural inspiration is to serve them in summer with a cooling Cucumber and Yogurt Salad (see Index), a dish found in both Greece and India.

½ cup milk
2 eggs, separated
½ cup all-purpose flour
½ cup freshly grated Parmesan cheese
½ teaspoon salt
Freshly ground black pepper, to taste
1 clove garlic, minced

1 tablespoon grated onion
2 tablespoons chopped fresh herbs
 of your choice (oregano, basil,
 thyme, parsley)
2 cups grated zucchini
 (about 1 medium)
¼ cup olive oil

1. Place the milk and egg yolks in a medium-size mixing bowl and stir well. Add the flour, Parmesan, salt, pepper, garlic, onion, and herbs. Mix well. Add the grated zucchini and mix well.

2. Pour the olive oil into a skillet or sauté pan and place it over medium heat. Place a serving platter in the oven and preheat to 200°F.

3. Beat the egg whites until they hold soft peaks. Fold the whites into the zucchini mixture carefully but thoroughly.

4. When the surface of the oil begins to ripple, scoop up a spoonful of batter with a large serving spoon and place it in the hot oil. Repeat until the pan is full. (A 9-inch pan will hold about three oblong [4 × 3-inch] pancakes.) Fry the pancakes until they are golden brown on the bottom, about 2 minutes; turn them with a metal spatula and brown on the other side as well, another 2 minutes. When the first batch is done, transfer them to the warm platter. Repeat until all of the batter is cooked, then serve immediately.

CHAPTER 7

FRUITS AND SWEETS

There's no squelching a sweet tooth craving! I was visiting some friends in California, and while there was invited to a barbecue. The dinner was a hearty one and our host, a Cuban–Puerto Rican friend of mine, had not prepared a dessert, much to the chagrin of his guests, myself included. There was a lot of joking around the table about whose sweet tooth is worse—Southerners' or Latin Americans'. Knowing my friend well, I knew that he had the makings for something sweet in his kitchen, even though he insisted that there was "nothing" there.

"Do you have tortillas?" I asked, knowing full well he did.

"Why, yes," he said hesitantly.

I pressed on. "Don't you have any ice cream? I've never known you to be without."

"Yes, but certainly not enough to go around." He hadn't a clue as to where I was heading.

"How about some lard?" I thought that might be pushing it, but it was worth a try; he *is* Cuban, after all.

"Well, yes, you know I do, but what on earth for?" He wondered aloud.

"I'll make fried ice cream. I know you have some jam; we'll melt it for the sauce." I was astounded at my own adamancy. "We'll roll up some ice cream in the tortillas and fry them in the lard and pour the sauce over them!"

Twenty minutes later, every morsel of this impromptu, nontraditional dessert had disappeared from every plate. We had satisfied our craving. (You'll find a crushed-vanilla-wafer-covered version of this creation in this chapter.)

My sweet tooth isn't as bad as it once was, but I do love the little fried doughs that are offered the world over at breakfast, tea, or after dinner. And I don't mind leaving the dinner table to fry dessert. It gives my guests a chance to relax a little, and when the frying is done, I return to the table with fritters and coffee, to the delight of the diners. Most of these recipes use a dough or batter; some can be made ahead of time, such as the Fried Peach Pies.

Three recipes for sweet sauces, which complement many dessert fritters, are included here as well. Besides the recipes included here, Chapter 2 includes several for fried breads, such as Sopaipillas and Crêpes, that take well to sweet sauces and fillings; be sure to check them out, too.

APPLE FRITTERS

SERVES 4

I grew up in a small South Carolina town that was settled early in the 18th century by Swiss and Germans. There's a wonderful legacy of cookie, torte, and fritter recipes in Orangeburg, as well as incomparable sausage-making skills. When I went fishing, I would go down to the local bakery at 6:00 A.M. for freshly glazed doughnuts to take with me. I've never had better. This recipe came from *Orangeburg's Choice Recipes,* published by the town's P.T.A. in 1948. The batter is equally delicious for fritters made with pears or plums.

3 large crisp eating apples, such as
    Granny Smith (see Note)
Juice of 1 lemon
3 tablespoons sugar, plus extra
    for dusting
¾ cup all-purpose flour
¼ teaspoon salt
2 large eggs, separated
½ cup water
1 teaspoon unsalted butter, melted
Peanut oil for deep-frying

1. Core and peel the apples. Slice them ⅓ inch thick, and place them in a bowl. Sprinkle with about 1 tablespoon of the lemon juice and the 3 tablespoons sugar. Toss well and allow to sit at room temperature for 30 minutes.

2. Sift the flour and salt together into a medium-size bowl. (Keep the sifter nearby.) Make a slight hollow in the center and add the egg yolks, 1 teaspoon lemon juice, and ¼ cup of the water. Mix with a wooden spoon. Then add the remaining ¼ cup water and the melted butter, beating hard and pressing the batter against the bowl to break up lumps.

3. Pour oil to a depth of 3 inches in a stockpot or Dutch oven, place it over medium heat, and heat it to 365°F.

4. While the oil is heating, beat the egg whites until they form stiff peaks. Fold them into the batter. Drain the apple slices in a sieve.

5. When the oil has reached 365°F, take a handful of apple slices and drop them into the batter to coat completely. Using your fingers, pick up one slice at a time and allow the excess batter to drain off before dropping it into the oil. Do not crowd the pot, and keep the temperature between 350° and 365°F. Cook until golden brown, about 3 minutes. Drain on paper towels and sprinkle with sifted sugar. Repeat with the remaining apple slices.

Note: Do not use baking apples for this recipe.

FRIED BANANAS

SERVES 4

Everyone loves fried bananas, a popular dessert throughout the tropical world. I adapted this recipe from one that my friend JoAnn Yaeger gave me. It's made with a rich *palacsinta* batter that reflects her Hungarian heritage. JoAnn coats hers with *panko*—very white bread crumbs from Japan, available at Asian groceries. Talk about a cross-cultural recipe!

If you can't find *panko,* store leftover baguettes in a paper bag and allow them to dry rock-hard. Grate them through the large holes of a hand grater. The large, dry crumbs will work just fine.

You can serve these banana fritters with ice cream, or with the chocolate sauce or fruit purées in this chapter. Spoon a pool of sauce on each plate or drizzle it all over the bananas.

Peanut oil for frying
½ **cup soft southern flour (see Note) or**
    cake flour
Pinch of salt
Pinch of sugar
1 large egg
½ **cup heavy (or whipping) cream**
1 tablespoon Grand Marnier
1 cup very fine dry bread crumbs
4 firm ripe bananas, peeled and halved

1. Pour oil to a depth of at least 2 inches in a large pot, place it over medium-high heat, and heat it to 365°F. Place a wire rack on a baking sheet, and set it aside.

2. While the oil is heating, prepare the batter: Stir the flour, salt, and sugar together in a medium-size bowl, and then make a well in the center. Add the egg and 2 tablespoons of the cream, and stir together with a wooden spoon, gradually adding the remaining cream until it is all incorporated into the batter. Stir in the Grand Marnier. Put the bread crumbs on a plate or in a shallow bowl.

3. When the oil reaches 365°F, dip the bananas in the batter, then into the bread crumbs. Pack the crumbs well onto the bananas. Fry the bananas until they are golden brown all over, 2 to 3 minutes. Do not crowd the pot,

and keep the temperature at 365°F. Transfer the bananas to the wire rack to drain.

4. Serve the bananas hot, with the sauce of your choice.

Note: Southern flour is made from soft winter wheat with a low gluten content. White Lily is a reliable brand. If you cannot find it in your area, write to White Lily at P.O. Box 871, Knoxville, TN 37901.

MADELEINE'S FIG BEIGNETS

SERVES 8 TO 12

Madeleine Kamman has taught traditional French culinary techniques to a whole generation of American chefs. I've heard several of them say that they learned more from Madeleine in two weeks than they did in several years of culinary school. I'm fortunate enough to count her among my friends. She sent me this "nice little thing" (her words), knowing that many of us in the South have backyard fig trees.

The figs that grow in the Deep South are very different from the Black Mission and Calimyrna figs of California. Our Brown Turkey and Celeste varieties are very soft-skinned, small, and delicate. If you are using fresh figs from California, make several slices in the flesh and fan the fruit out a bit. If you're using southern figs (which are too soft to ship), you may want to use very firm or underripe ones, or eliminate the fanning.

Peanut oil for deep-frying
1¾ cups all-purpose flour, sifted
2 pints (16 to 32) figs, ripe but
    not oozing juice
2 eggs, separated
¼ teaspoon salt
3 tablespoons granulated sugar
¾ to 1 cup milk
Confectioners' sugar, for dusting

1. Pour oil to a depth of 3 to 4 inches in a large pot or Dutch oven, place it over medium heat, and heat it to 365°F. Place some crumpled paper towels on a plate or baking sheet, and set it aside. Place ¼ cup of the flour in a shallow bowl.

2. While the oil is heating, prepare the figs: If you are using California or underripe south-

ern figs, slice them into fans: Place the figs on a cutting board. Holding each fig by the stem end, make several slices along its length, all the way through the fig but stopping short of the stem; press lightly to fan out. Dust each fig well with flour, shaking off any excess.

3. In a medium-size mixing bowl, make a batter by mixing together the remaining 1½ cups flour, the egg yolks, salt, granulated sugar, and milk. Beat the egg whites until they form soft peaks, and fold them into the batter.

4. Dip the figs into the batter and then drop them into the hot oil, frying each one until golden brown, 2 to 3 minutes. Do not crowd the pot and keep the temperature at 365°F. Remove the figs from the pot, letting any excess oil drain off into the pot, and place them on the paper towels to drain. Dust with confectioners' sugar before serving.

FRIED PEACH PIES

SERVES 3 TO 6

If you've never fried pies before, give this recipe a try. These turnovers, filled with peaches seasoned with a hint of cinnamon, are better than baked. This is an old-fashioned southern treat that deserves to be revived. The recipe makes six pies, ample for as many people, but I've seen some people eat two or three of them at one sitting! Plan accordingly.

4 firm ripe peaches (about 1 pound)
¼ cup sugar
1 to 2 tablespoons fresh lemon juice
¼ teaspoon ground cinnamon
1¼ cups self-rising flour
⅓ cup unsalted butter or lard, chilled
¼ cup ice water
Peanut oil for deep-frying
Sugar, for dusting (optional)

1. To make the peaches easy to peel, drop them into a pot of boiling water and let them cook for about a minute. Then peel them, pit them, and cube them. You should have 2 cups of cut fruit.

2. Put the peaches, ¼ cup sugar, lemon juice, and cinnamon in a nonreactive sauté pan and stir to dissolve the sugar. Cook over

low to medium heat, stirring occasionally, until the mixture resembles chunky applesauce and the liquid is very thick, 20 to 30 minutes. Do not let the sugar caramelize. Turn the mixture out onto a plate or into a bowl, and place it in the refrigerator to cool.

3. In the meantime, make the dough: Sift the flour into a large mixing bowl with slanting sides. Cut the butter into small pieces and add them to the flour. Using a pastry blender or two knives, work the butter into the flour. When it is incorporated uniformly, drizzle the ice water into the flour as you toss it with a large slotted spoon. Then, using your hands, form the dough, which will be crumbly, into a ball. Wrap the dough well in plastic wrap or wax paper, and refrigerate it for at least 30 minutes.

4. You can make the pies (step 5) ahead of time and chill them before frying, or you can make them while the oil heats and fry them as soon as they are made. If you are proceeding directly with the recipe, pour oil to a depth of 3 to 4 inches in a stockpot or Dutch oven, place it over medium-high heat, and heat it to 375°F. While it is heating, prepare the pies.

5. Remove the dough and the peach filling from the refrigerator. On a lightly floured surface, roll out the dough to form a rough rectangle. Fold each side in toward the center so that you have square corners. Roll the dough out to form an 8 × 12-inch rectangle. With a knife, slice the rectangle into six 4-inch squares. Place a heaping tablespoon of filling in the center of each square, and paint a ¼-inch band of water along two adjacent edges of the square. Fold the opposite corner over to form a triangular turnover, lining the edges up perfectly. Seal the edges together well with the tines of a fork. If you're planning to fry the pies immediately, monitor the temperature of the oil while you are making the six pies; it should not go over 375°F. If you are going to fry the pies later, use a metal spatula to lift them carefully and transfer them to a plate; cover with plastic wrap, and refrigerate for up to 6 hours.

6. When you are ready to fry the pies, have ready some crumpled paper towels, and a shallow bowl of sugar for dusting, if desired. Fry three pies at a time. If they are room-temperature, do not let the oil drop below 365°F. If the pies are chilled, preheat the oil to 390°F, and do not let it drop below 370°F. Fry the pies until golden brown all over, about 3 minutes. Use a wire mesh strainer to lower and raise them. Remove the pies, letting excess oil drip back into the pot, and place them on the paper towels to drain. Repeat the process with the remaining pies. Then roll the pies in sugar, if desired.

STUFFED PRUNES

SERVES 4

This bit of Austrian decadence was adapted from a recipe in Olga and Adolf Hess's cookbook *Viennese Cooking,* first translated and published in the United States in 1952. It reminds me of the sort of sugar extravaganzas we prided ourselves on in college, when I could eat two huge bowls of ice cream without so much as thinking about it.

1 pound large pitted prunes
¼ cup rum, or more as needed
1 cup blanched whole almonds, or
    enough to stuff the prunes
1 cup milk
1⅓ cups all-purpose flour
2 large eggs
3 tablespoons sugar
Dash of salt
Peanut oil for deep-frying
¾ cup grated semisweet chocolate

1. Six hours or the night before you plan to serve the dessert, place the prunes in a saucepan, cover them with water, bring to a boil, and then remove from the heat. Allow them to sit for 10 minutes, then pour off the water. Cover the prunes with the rum and leave them at room temperature until you're ready to cook them.

2. Place a sieve over a bowl, and strain the prunes, reserving the rum. Place an almond inside each prune.

3. In a medium-size bowl, stir the milk, flour, and eggs together well. Add 1 tablespoon of the sugar and 1 tablespoon of the reserved rum (add more rum if there isn't a full tablespoon). Add the salt and mix well.

4. Pour oil to a depth of 3 inches in a stockpot or Dutch oven, place it over medium-high heat, and heat it to 365°F. Line a colander with crumpled paper towels and set it near the stove. Mix the chocolate with the remaining sugar, and spread on a baking sheet lined with wax paper.

5. When the oil reaches 365°F, drop five or six prunes into the batter. Then use tongs to lift them from the batter, letting any excess drip off, and lower them into the oil. Do not crowd the pot, and keep the oil between 350° and 365°F. Fry the fritters until golden, 3 to 4 minutes, then transfer them to the prepared colander. Pat them dry of excess oil, then roll them, while hot, in the chocolate mixture. Continue with the rest of the prunes, then serve.

ELDERBERRY-FLOWER FRITTERS

SERVES 6

Tall wild elderberry bushes (*Sambucus canadensis* and *S. caerulea*) grow in roadside ditches from Canada to the Gulf of Mexico. When their snowy white blossoms open in early summer, I like to pick some and make this recipe, which comes from the Alps. The elderberry blossoms are very sweet and fragrant, but the leaves, bark, branches, and roots are poisonous. Even the berry cannot be eaten raw, though the European variety is the major ingredient in the popular licorice-flavored Italian liqueur, Sambuca.

If elderberries grow near you, try to harvest the flowers either very early in the morning or just before cooking. If you pick them early in the day, cut long stems and put them in a bucket of water in a cool spot until you're ready to cook; if you're going directly into the kitchen, pick each cluster with a two-inch piece of stem and place the umbrella-like clusters in a large paper sack. Do not wash the flowers, but check them carefully for insects. Each diner gets one flower cluster.

The traditional garnish is a dollop of Swiss elderberry jam, but you can also use the fruit purées at the end of this chapter.

1 cup sweet white wine from
    Germany, Alsace, Switzerland,
    or Austria, or 1 cup dry white wine
2 teaspoons granulated sugar
    (for dry wine)
1½ cups all-purpose flour
1 teaspoon grated lemon zest
Dash of salt
2 large egg whites
Peanut oil for deep-frying
6 fresh elderberry-flower clusters
Confectioners' sugar, for dusting

1. Pour the wine into a large bowl. If you're using a dry wine, add the granulated sugar. Stir the flour into the wine with a whisk, beating until there are no lumps. Stir in the lemon zest and salt.

2. Pour oil to a depth of 3 inches in a stockpot or Dutch oven, place it over medium heat, and heat to 350°F. Place a wire rack on a baking sheet and set it near the stove.

3. While the oil is heating, beat the egg whites until they hold stiff peaks. Then gently but thoroughly fold them into the batter. Using scissors, trim the stem below each flower cluster to a 1-inch length.

4. When the oil reaches 350°F, dip each cluster into the batter, holding it by the stem. Raise the cluster and let any excess batter drip off, but make sure that all the flowers and their tiny stems are coated. Carefully lower the cluster into the hot oil, and fry until it is golden brown, about 3 minutes. Lift the fritter out of the batter with a wire mesh strainer, or by using tongs to pick it up by the stem. Place the fritter on the wire rack and continue frying the remaining clusters.

5. Serve immediately, turning the fritters right side up and dusting them with confectioners' sugar.

TINA'S FRITTERS

SERVES 6

Sfingi (sphinxes) is what Sicilians call these little fried puffs of sweetened dough. They *can* look like sphinxes, but they can just as easily take on the shape of a dog, cat, or hippopotamus. Tina Cerasoli, whose daughter Celia's eponymous restaurant in Charleston serves up traditional southern Italian fare, taught me their family version. Celia says part of the fun of making them as a child was to watch the fritters take on the shapes as they entered the oil—sort of a culinary Rorschach test. Every Sicilian-American I know has a different recipe, many of them for a buttery cream-puff paste. This is a simplified version of Tina's, which involves repeatedly spanking the dough "like a baby's bottom." Family members take turns at the mixing, pulling the sticky dough from each other's hands with squeezing handshakes.

Sfingi are traditionally served on March 19, St. Joseph's Day; another version, made with a cream-puff dough, is filled with a sweet orange cream. Tina's version is lighter than most; she says you can add as many or few raisins as you like. They might sink to the bottom of the dough, but that's okay: the last ones fried will be those with the raisins.

You can also mix the dough in an electric mixer with a paddle attachment, beating well until the dough is smooth. Just don't tell Tina!

1½ teaspoons active dry yeast
¼ cup warm water (110°F)
2 cups all-purpose flour
¼ cup plus 3 tablespoons sugar
½ teaspoon salt
¾ cup water
1 large egg, lightly beaten
½ cup raisins (optional)
Peanut oil for deep-frying
1 teaspoon ground cinnamon

1. In a small bowl, dissolve the yeast in the warm water and allow it to proof for about 10 minutes, or until it is creamy and slightly bubbly.

2. Sift together the flour, ¼ cup sugar, and salt into a large mixing bowl. Make a well in the center, and add the proofed yeast and the ¾ cup water. Mix the dough with one hand, holding the bowl steady with the other, until it is smooth and elastic. Then add the egg and mix it in well.

3. Beat the dough with the palm and fingers of your hand, continually "spanking" it. ("Your shoulders and elbows need to be loose," Celia explains. "I cradle the bowl in one arm and slap the dough with the other hand.") Continue until the dough is silky and little bubbles are beginning to appear on the surface. It will take about 15 minutes by hand.

4. Sprinkle the raisins, if using, evenly over the dough, then mix well one last time. Cover the bowl with a towel and allow it to rest, away from drafts, for about 2 hours, or until the dough has doubled in size.

5. Pour oil to a depth of 3 inches in a stockpot or Dutch oven, place it over medium-high heat, and heat it to 375°F. Mix the cinnamon and 3 tablespoons sugar together in a shallow bowl and set aside. Place a wire rack on a baking sheet and set it aside.

6. When the oil reaches 375°F, dip a teaspoon into the edge of the dough and scoop up a little ball of dough. Using a second teaspoon, scrape the ball off the spoon and into the hot oil. Continue taking spoonfuls from the edge of the dough, being careful not to deflate it, and adding them to the oil. Carefully monitor the oil temperature, maintaining it between 365° and 375°F; do not crowd the pot. Fry the fritters until they are golden all over, turning them if necessary, 3 to 4 minutes. Transfer to wire racks to drain. Before serving, toss them in the cinnamon sugar, dusting off any excess.

SWEET FRIED RICOTTA

SERVES 6

Like the preceding recipe for Tina's Fritters, these, too, might be called *sfingi* in Sicily. They would be made with thick, fresh ricotta in Italy, but the American-made ricotta that's available in supermarkets works well here. Look for an all-natural brand, made from whole milk. Serve these in the afternoon with a glass of Marsala.

1 pint (2 cups) ricotta cheese
2 tablespoons superfine sugar
1 teaspoon vanilla extract
1 teaspoon grated lemon zest
1 teaspoon ground cinnamon
3 tablespoons, more or less,
    self-rising flour
Peanut oil for frying
Confectioners' sugar or honey,
    for serving

1. Mix the ricotta, superfine sugar, vanilla, lemon zest, and cinnamon in a medium-size bowl. Add the flour a little at a time, stirring, until the mixture is fairly stiff.

2. Pour oil to a depth of 2 inches in a stockpot or Dutch oven, place it over medium-high heat, and heat it to 365°F. Line a baking sheet with paper towels and place it near the stove.

3. When the oil reaches 365°F, begin dropping the dough by tablespoonfuls into the oil, cooking several at a time. Maintain the temperature between 350° and 365°F. Cook until golden brown all over, about 4 minutes. Remove with tongs or a wire mesh strainer, and place on the paper towels to drain. When all the ricotta is fried, dust the fritters with confectioners' sugar or drizzle honey over them, and serve immediately.

AZOREAN DREAMS

MAKES ABOUT 32

Oranges, lemons, and pineapples grow in the Azores, 900 miles west of the Portuguese mainland. Azoreans are a very religious people, but their Mardi Gras feasts are elaborate and bacchanalian. A favorite Mardi Gras feature are these eggy *sonhos* (dreams), glazed in an orange syrup; they are a lovely version of cream-puff fritters.

Pâte à choux—choux, or cream-puff, pastry—is one of the most versatile doughs and is not difficult to make. It appears in dozens of permutations throughout the world's kitchens, including this version from the Azores, in which it is dropped by spoonfuls into hot oil and fried. The lovely irregular puffs of the rich dough can be dusted with confectioners' sugar and served with a fruit purée. Or you can add grated Parmesan to the batter for a savory fritter; dust extra cheese on the warm fritters before passing them when you're serving cocktails. Offer a glass of Madeira with this sweet version.

1 cup water
6 tablespoons (¾ stick) unsalted butter
½ teaspoon salt
Zest of 1 lemon, peeled in a single strip
1 cup all-purpose flour
4 or 5 large eggs
1 cup sugar
½ cup fresh orange juice
Peanut oil for deep-frying

1. Combine the water, butter, salt, and lemon zest in a saucepan and place over medium heat until the butter melts. Remove the zest, raise the heat, and bring the mixture to a boil. Immediately remove from the heat and pour in the flour all at once, stirring with a wooden spoon. Stop when the mixture forms a ball. Set it aside to cool for a few minutes.

2. Break 4 eggs into a measuring cup with a pouring lip and, if necessary, add enough egg white from the fifth egg to measure exactly 1 cup.

3. Place the dough in a food processor. With the machine running, add about one egg at a time, mixing well after each addition. Let the mixture rest for 10 minutes.

4. While the dough is resting, combine the sugar and orange juice in a saucepan and bring to a boil over low heat; boil until a thick syrup is formed, 10 to 15 minutes. Remove the pan from the heat, but keep it on the stove to stay warm while you fry the dreams. Place a double layer of paper towels on a baking sheet, and set it near the stove.

5. Pour oil into a stockpot or Dutch oven to a depth of at least 2 inches, and heat it over medium-high heat to 365°F. Drop the batter by tablespoonfuls into the oil and fry until golden, about 2 minutes. Remove the dreams from the oil, drain them on the paper towels, and then dip them in the hot glaze. Serve immediately.

BEIGNETS

MAKES 16

Beignet is French for "fritter"; the word is Celtic in origin. In France, the word refers to any food dipped in batter and fried, but in New Orleans, beignets are square doughnuts without holes. They are sold every day by the thousands at the old Café du Monde in the French Quarter.

Make these just before you serve them, for breakfast, with big cups of café au lait. In New Orleans, café au lait is made with twice-boiled milk, a technique that sweetens the milk: Bring milk to a boil, remove from the heat, and bring to a boil again. Strain it into cups or mugs, mixing it with equal parts of very strong coffee.

1 package active dry yeast
¼ cup warm water (110°F)
2 tablespoons granulated sugar
2 tablespoons unsalted butter
½ cup heavy (or whipping) cream
1 large egg
4 cups all-purpose flour
Peanut oil for deep-frying
Confectioners' sugar, for dusting

1. In a large bowl, dissolve the yeast in the warm water and allow to proof for about 10 minutes. It should become creamy and slightly bubbly.

2. Meanwhile, place the sugar, butter, and cream in a small saucepan and heat over low heat until the butter melts. Remove from the heat and allow to cool to lukewarm.

3. Beat the egg into the cream mixture. Then pour the mixture into the yeast and mix well. Add 2 cups of the flour and mix well, beating with a wooden spoon. Add another cup of flour and beat smooth again, then continue adding flour until the dough is no longer sticky. Add only as much flour as is necessary. Gather the dough into a ball and place it on a lightly floured work surface.

4. Pour oil to a depth of 3 inches in a Dutch oven or stockpot, place it over medium heat, and heat it to 365°F. Place a wire rack on a baking sheet and set it near the stove.

5. While the oil is heating, dust a rolling pin with flour and lightly roll the dough out, turning it a quarter-turn, rolling it out some more, then turning it another quarter-turn, until you have a 16-inch square about ¼ inch thick. Cut the dough into sixteen 4-inch squares.

6. When the oil reaches 365°F, lift the squares up with a spatula and drop two or three at a time into the oil. They will probably sink to the bottom of the pot. As soon as they rise to the surface (or when the underside is brown), turn them over and fry until crisp on the other side, about 3 minutes in all. Transfer them to the wire rack, and continue frying the rest of the beignets, carefully maintaining the temperature between 360° and 370°F. Dust the drained beignets with confectioners' sugar, and serve immediately.

DOUGHNUTS

MAKES ABOUT 24 DOUGHNUTS AND HOLES

Old-fashioned raised doughnuts are very easy to make. The dough is a yeast dough enriched with an egg and a little milk; it's very loose, so the doughnuts will puff up in the hot fat. Unlike most yeast doughs, you don't need to work this one very much. You'll need a doughnut cutter or two biscuit cutters, one 3 inches in diameter and one 1 inch in diameter.

1 package active dry yeast
¼ cup warm water (110°F)
3 to 4 cups all-purpose flour
2 tablespoons granulated
  sugar
½ teaspoon salt
4 tablespoons (½ stick)
  unsalted butter
¾ cup milk
1 large egg

Vegetable oil for deep-frying
Confectioners' sugar, cinnamon sugar,
  or sugar glaze (see box, page 154)

1. In a small bowl, dissolve the yeast in the warm water; set it aside to proof for about 10 minutes. It should become creamy and slightly bubbly.

2. Warm a large mixing bowl; then sift 3 cups of the flour with the sugar and salt into it.

3. Heat the butter and milk in a small saucepan over low heat until the butter melts. Remove the pan from the heat. When the milk is no longer hot (under 120°F), mix it with the yeast. Beat the egg into the yeast mixture.

4. Make a well in the center of the flour, and add the yeast mixture, beating with your hand or a wooden spoon until a smooth dough is formed, and adding additional flour until the dough is no longer sticky. Turn the dough out onto a lightly floured surface, and knead it for about 5 minutes. Then form the dough into a ball, invert the mixing bowl over the dough, and allow it to rise until doubled in bulk, about 1 hour.

5. Roll the dough out about ⅜ inch thick. Using a floured doughnut cutter or two biscuit cutters, cut out the doughnuts. Reroll the scraps and cut out more doughnuts. Cover the doughnuts and the "holes" with a tea towel, and allow to rise again until doubled, 30 to 45 minutes.

6. Pour oil to a depth of 3 inches in a Dutch oven or stockpot, place it over medium-high heat, and heat to 365°F. Place a wire rack on a baking sheet and set it near the stove.

7. When the oil reaches 365°F, carefully scoop up the doughnuts with a metal spatula so they don't lose their shape, and fry them in the oil, several at a time, until golden brown, about 1 minute on each side. Do not let the temperature drop below 360°F or the doughnuts will absorb oil. Transfer them from the oil to the wire rack to drain. Continue the process until all the doughnuts and holes are fried. Dust with confectioners' sugar, roll in cinnamon sugar, or dip in a sugar glaze and return to the rack to dry.

COATINGS FOR DOUGHNUTS

To finish off your doughnuts, sprinkle on cinnamon sugar or top them with a glaze.

Cinnamon sugar is made by mixing 1 teaspoon ground cinnamon with 3 tablespoons sugar. I usually roll the holes in cinnamon sugar and dust the doughnuts with confectioners' sugar. Or sometimes I dip them in a glaze made by mixing 1 cup confectioners' sugar with 2 tablespoons milk.

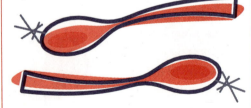

FRENCH MARVELS

MAKES 24 TO 36

Wherever the French settled in America, you can find a variation of these fried cookies. The French call them *merveilles* (marvels); in Louisiana they cut them in the shape of pigs' ears and call them just that (*oreilles de cochon*). The recipe hasn't changed in two hundred years. Try them and you'll see why.

The French dust marvels with vanilla sugar, which you can make by leaving a vanilla bean in a sugar canister so it flavors the sugar. In Louisiana, they pour cane syrup over them. I'm partial to a simple dusting with confectioners' sugar. You can serve one of the fruit purées in this chapter with them as well if you like. These make a wonderful breakfast, served with café au lait.

2¾ cups all-purpose flour
Pinch of salt
8 tablespoons (1 stick) unsalted butter,
    cold
1 tablespoon granulated sugar
3 large eggs
Peanut oil for deep-frying
Confectioners' sugar, for dusting

1. Sift the flour and salt together into a large mixing bowl with sloping sides. Cut in the butter, using a pastry blender or two knives, until it is evenly incorporated.

2. Lightly beat the granulated sugar into the eggs in a small bowl, and then add it to the flour mixture and blend well with a wooden spoon. If the dough is dry or crumbly, pick it up in your hands and press it all together lightly into a ball. Do not knead. Wrap it well in plastic wrap and refrigerate for 1 hour.

3. Pour oil to a depth of at least 2 inches in a stockpot or Dutch oven, place it over medium-high heat, and heat it to 375°F. Place a wire rack on a baking sheet and set it near the stove.

4. While the oil is heating, roll out the dough on a lightly floured surface with a lightly floured rolling pin into as thin a sheet as possible and cut it into whatever cookie shapes you want. You should wind up with between two and three dozen.

5. When the oil reaches 375°F, begin dropping the marvels into the hot oil without crowding the pot, and fry until golden brown, 2 to 5 minutes depending on the thickness of the cookies. Keep the oil between 365° and 375°F. Transfer the cookies to the wire rack to drain, and then dust them with confectioners' sugar. Serve immediately.

CALAS

SERVES 6

Wherever rice is grown, you can find rice fritters, both sweet and savory. In Italy they tuck some cheese and ham in them; in China they're likely to include some dried shrimp. Sweet fried rice balls are also common, though few are made like these—with an overnight leaven. Even in New Orleans, where this version originated, baking powder has replaced the traditional yeast. These delicious little fritters—*beignets de riz*—deserved to be revived. They are a perfect example of how African cooks adopted a French technique and transformed traditional West African rice cakes (called calas from *cala,* an African word for rice) into a new Creole dish. Make up the leaven the night before, then fry them fresh for a traditional Creole breakfast, served with big cups of café au lait.

2¼ cups cold water
¾ cup long-grain white rice
1 teaspoon salt
1 package active dry yeast
½ cup warm water (110°F)
4 large eggs
⅓ cup granulated sugar
½ teaspoon freshly grated nutmeg
2¼ cups all-purpose flour
Peanut oil for deep-frying
Confectioners' sugar, for dusting

1. The night before you plan to serve, combine the cold water, rice, and salt in a saucepan and bring to a boil over medium-high heat. As soon as it boils, turn the heat down and simmer, uncovered, until the rice is mushy, 30 minutes. Drain off any excess water, then place the rice in a large bowl and mash it thoroughly. Let the rice cool to lukewarm.

2. Meanwhile, in a small bowl, dissolve the yeast in the warm water and let it sit for about 10 minutes. It should be creamy and bubbly. When the rice has cooled, stir the yeast mixture into it, beating with a wooden spoon to make sure it is mixed in well. Cover the bowl with plastic wrap and let it sit at room temperature overnight.

3. About 45 minutes before serving time, add the eggs, granulated sugar, and nutmeg to the rice and stir in well. Gradually add the flour, beating hard with a wooden spoon until all the flour is incorporated. Cover the bowl again and allow it to sit for 30 minutes.

4. When the rice mixture has been sitting for about 25 minutes, pour oil to a depth of 3 inches in a stockpot or Dutch oven, place it over medium-high heat, and heat it to 375°F.

Preheat the oven to 200°F. Place a wire rack on a baking sheet, and set it in the oven.

5. When the oil reaches 375°F, use two tablespoons to form the calas: one to scoop up a heaping spoonful and the other to scrape it off quickly into the oil. Cook three or four at a time, avoiding crowding the pot and carefully maintaining the temperature between 365° and 375°F. Fry the calas until golden brown on both sides, about 3 minutes total. Remove them from the oil with a wire mesh strainer, and place them on the wire rack to drain and stay warm while you cook the remaining dough. Serve warm, dusted with confectioners' sugar.

FRIED ICE CREAM

SERVES 8

This is a wonderful dessert for a children's party—for the adults as well as the kids! The dish is infinitely variable because you can use whatever ice cream, coatings, and sauces you wish. You may want to adjust your freezer so that it's colder than normal and put these in the coldest area—they have to be deeply frozen for the recipe to work. Start at least one day in advance.

Count on eight servings from a quart of ice cream. Professional ice cream scoops are graded; you'll want to use a No. 8 (½ cup). If you don't have a scoop, divide the quart into ½-cup servings and shape them into balls with your hands (wear rubber gloves if it's too cold for you). If the coating is too thin, freeze the ice cream balls and coat them a second time.

1 cup finely chopped pecans
1 quart vanilla ice cream
1 large egg
2 cups crushed vanilla wafers
Peanut oil for deep-frying
Double recipe Chocolate
    Sauce (page 158)

1. Place the chopped nuts in a shallow bowl. Line a baking sheet (that will fit in your freezer) with wax paper.

2. Divide the ice cream into eight ½-cup scoops and

157

shape them into perfect balls (see headnote). Roll each ice cream ball in the nuts and place it on the prepared baking sheet. Place the ice cream balls in the freezer until frozen very hard, at least 3 hours.

3. Beat the egg in a shallow bowl, and place the crushed wafers in another shallow bowl. Roll each ice cream ball in the egg , then in the wafers, making sure that the ball is completely encased. Freeze the balls again until very hard, about 3 hours more.

4. When you are ready to serve the dessert, pour oil to a depth of 3 inches in a stockpot or Dutch oven, place it over medium-high heat, and heat it to 375°F. Place a wire rack on a baking sheet, and set it near the stove.

5. When the oil reaches 375°F, take the ice cream balls out of the freezer and fry several balls at a time until the coating is crisp, about 30 seconds. Transfer them to the wire rack to drain, and then serve them right away, with the chocolate sauce.

CHOCOLATE SAUCE

SERVES 4

This simple sauce is an elegant garnish for fritters. Use the best chocolate you can find and a mild-flavored honey. The recipe will make enough to garnish four servings, such as the Fried Bananas; it may be doubled. It takes only minutes to make.

**2 ounces high-quality semisweet
chocolate**
**2 to 3 tablespoons heavy
(or whipping) cream**
**1 tablespoon mild-flavored
honey, such as clover**

Combine all the ingredients in a small saucepan over very low

heat, stirring until well blended. Use immediately by pouring a pool of the sauce on each dessert plate (to be topped by fritters, for example) or by dipping the tines of a fork into the sauce and drizzling sauce all over the fritters and the plate.

RASPBERRY SAUCE

SERVES 4

Pour a pool of this brightly colored sauce on dessert plates before adding a mound of dessert fritters. If you're using frozen berries in syrup, omit the sugar.

1 cup fresh raspberries, or 1 package
    (10 ounces) frozen raspberries in
    syrup, thawed
2 to 3 tablespoons superfine sugar
    (if using fresh berries)
2 tablespoons fresh lemon juice
2 tablespoons raspberry liqueur,
    such as framboise or Chambord

1. Put the berries in a blender and purée them. If you are using fresh berries, add the sugar, to taste, and blend again.

2. Strain the purée through a nonreactive sieve to remove the seeds. Stir in the lemon juice and liqueur. Serve at room temperature or chilled.

FRUIT SAUCES

Puréed fruits make delicious sauces for dessert fritters. Some soft fruits, such as raspberries, can be made into a pourable sauce by simply blending and straining them; others need to be poached first to make them soft enough to purée. Generally speaking, you can purée any fruit by preparing it as you would for eating, then straining it. If it needs to be softened, cook it a little first. Fruit sauces are often flavored with sugar, honey, or other fruit juices; spirits or spices can be added as well.

The two recipes here are quick and simple, and their clean flavors nicely complement fritter batters. One can be made with frozen berries; the other features tropical mangoes. The acids in fruits will react with aluminum, iron, and copper, so be sure to use stainless-steel, glass, or plastic bowls and stainless or plastic sieves.

MANGO PUREE

SERVES 4

This lovely purée is a staple of today's new American chefs. It is delicious with fruit, with chicken, and with dessert fritters.

1 large ripe mango (about 1 pound)
1 to 2 tablespoons fresh orange juice
1 tablespoon rum (optional)
1 tablespoon honey, preferably orange
    blossom, or to taste

1. Place a large nonreactive sieve over a bowl. Peel and pit the mango over the sieve as best you can, letting the flesh drop into the sieve. Don't worry if you make mush of the fruit, as you're going to purée it anyway. Discard the seed and skin.

2. Press the fruit through the sieve to purée. Add the remaining ingredients, to taste, and stir well. Serve at room temperature.

CHAPTER 8

GO-WITHS

While many chips and fritters can stand on their own as appetizers, most meals of fried foods are incomplete without the dips, sauces, and purées that traditionally accompany them. No New Orleans chef is without mayonnaise and its variations, tartar sauce and rémoulade; fiery hot sauces are perennial favorites; and Asian dipping sauces are gaining popularity as a global cuisine emerges.

This chapter includes recipes for the foods that go with the dishes in this book: hollandaise sauces, red pepper purée, fresh salsas for chips and fritters, and a cocktail sauce for shrimp—perfect "go-withs"! And every fry cook needs a good recipe for potato salad and coleslaw. What better way to accompany fried chicken or fish?

Sweet fruit and chocolate sauces are with the desserts in Chapter 7.

SAUCES

BLENDER MAYONNAISE

MAKES ABOUT 1¼ CUPS

You can add special flavor to mayonnaise by using different oils: The leftover oil from a jar of sun-dried tomatoes makes an orange-colored mayonnaise that is delicious on crab cakes. Mayonnaise made with basil-infused oil is delicious with tomatoes. You can also add 1 to 3 tablespoons chopped herbs of your choice.

1 teaspoon prepared mustard
¼ teaspoon salt
Cayenne pepper, to taste (optional)
1 large egg (see box, facing page), at
    room temperature
1 cup peanut oil, or a blend of peanut
    and olive oils
1 tablespoon fresh lemon juice

1. Place the mustard, salt, cayenne, if using, and egg in a blender and blend on high speed for about 15 seconds.

2. Begin drizzling in the oil very slowly, in droplets at first, and blend until all of the oil is bound with the egg and the mayonnaise is thick and creamy.

3. With the motor off, scrape down the sides of the blender with a rubber spatula. Then add the lemon juice and blend quickly to incorporate.

4. Correct the seasoning if necessary. The mayonnaise can be stored, tightly covered, in the refrigerator for up to 1 week.

RED REMOULADE

MAKES ABOUT 1½ CUPS

Sauce *rémoulade* is a mayonnaise variation that traditionally accompanies eggs and fried fish as well as cold meats, shellfish, poultry, and vegetables. In New Orleans it's likely to contain some tomato and red pepper sauce rather than the traditional pickles and anchovies. It's a delicious part of the Upperline's Fried Green Tomatoes with Shrimp Rémoulade (see Index).

Blender Mayonnaise (facing page)
1 scant teaspoon Creole or
    Dijon mustard
1 scant tablespoon Worcestershire
    sauce
1½ tablespoons prepared or
    freshly grated horseradish
3 tablespoons mixed chopped
    fresh herbs of your choice
    (parsley, chervil, and tarragon
    are traditional)
2 teaspoons minced garlic
1 tablespoon grated white onion
2 tablespoons finely chopped scallion
    (including the green tops)
1½ tablespoons tomato paste
1 tablespoon Tabasco or other
    bottled hot pepper sauce,
    or to taste

Mix all the ingredients together well; then correct the seasoning to taste. You can leave the rémoulade rough or purée it to a smooth consistency in a blender.

MAYONNAISE SAUCES

Homemade mayonnaise is delicious, easy to make, infinitely variable, and an invaluable resource for fry cooks. It is made with raw eggs, but rather than fear salmonella poisoning (which is both rare and almost always occurs in an institutional setting such as a hotel or at a conference), the prudent cook should be aware of the provenance of eggs. Nearly every box of eggs sold in the United States has a toll-free number on it, as well as the batch number and expiration date, so that you can easily find out if the supplier has had an outbreak. Few have.

TARTAR SAUCE

MAKES ABOUT 1½ CUPS

Blender Mayonnaise (page 162)
1 tablespoon finely chopped sweet
  pickle, rinsed and drained
1 tablespoon capers, rinsed and
  drained
1 tablespoon minced onion
  or shallot
1 tablespoon minced fresh chervil,
  parsley, or dill

Combine all the ingredients and mix well.
Serve immediately,
with fried fish or
shellfish.

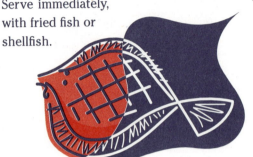

GARLIC MAYONNAISE (AIOLI)

MAKES ABOUT 1¼ CUPS

Blender Mayonnaise (page 162),
  prepared without mustard
4 cloves garlic, minced
1 to 3 tablespoons chopped
  mixed fresh herbs

Combine all of the ingredients and mix
well. Serve immediately, with fritters
(such as the Fried Baby Artichokes
on page 106 and the Black-Eyed Pea
Cakes on page 107).

HOLLANDAISE

MAKES ABOUT 1½ CUPS

3 large egg yolks
2 tablespoons lemon juice
Salt and freshly ground black pepper,
    to taste
1 cup (2 sticks) unsalted butter, cut into
    16 pieces

1. In a nonreactive wide bowl that will fit snugly over a saucepan, or in the nonreactive top of a double boiler, whisk the yolks with 1 tablespoon of the lemon juice and a little of the salt and pepper until just blended.

2. Place the bowl over simmering water, and whisking continuously, add the butter bit by bit, making sure each is well incorporated before adding another piece. Scrape the sides of the bowl as you whisk, and be sure that the eggs don't scramble. (If they should, you can try to save the sauce by picking up the bowl and quickly whisking in a spoonful of hot water—you can take it from the simmering water.) Continue whisking until all the butter is mixed in and the sauce is velvety smooth.

3. Remove the pan from the heat, but leave the bowl or double boiler top over the water so the sauce will stay warm. Adjust the seasoning to taste with the remaining lemon juice and salt and pepper, and whisk it occasionally as it stands to prevent it from breaking or forming a skin.

HOLLANDAISE SAUCES

Hollandaise is a luxurious combination of egg yolks and butter—a rich, warm cousin of mayonnaise. It is a hallmark of classic French cuisine. Hollandaise most often appears with poached fish, eggs, or vegetables, but when loosened with a bit of cream, the resulting Mousseline (page 166), nicely complements Salmon Croquettes. Thick and tangy Béarnaise (page 167), flavored with tarragon vinegar and shallots, teams with heartier foods such as Fried Lamb Patties. Sauce Choron (page 168) is a reddish béarnaise flavored with tomato instead of tarragon; it's used with the extravagant soft-shell crabs that Chef Jamie Shannon serves at Commander's Palace in New Orleans.

MOUSSELINE

MAKES ABOUT 1¼ CUPS

3 large egg yolks
2 tablespoons lemon juice
½ teaspoon salt
8 tablespoons (1 stick) unsalted
    butter, cut into 8 pieces
½ cup heavy (or whipping) cream
Cayenne pepper, to taste

1. In a nonreactive wide bowl that will fit snugly over a saucepan, or in the nonreactive top of a double boiler, whisk the yolks with 1 tablespoon of the lemon juice and the salt until just blended.

2. Place the bowl over simmering water, and whisking continuously, add the butter bit by bit, making sure each is well incorporated before adding another piece. Scrape the sides of the bowl as you whisk, and be sure that the eggs don't scramble. (If they should, you can try to save the sauce by picking up the bowl and quickly whisking in a spoonful of hot water—you can take it from the simmering water.)

Continue whisking until all the butter is mixed in and the sauce is velvety smooth.

3. Remove the pan from the heat, but leave the bowl or double boiler top over the water. Whisk in the cream; then adjust the seasoning to taste with the remaining lemon juice and the cayenne.

4. Set the sauce aside to stay warm while you prepare the main dish. Whisk it occasionally as it stands to prevent it from breaking or forming a skin.

BEARNAISE

MAKES ABOUT 1½ CUPS

1 cup white wine vinegar, or ¾ cup
    dry white wine plus ¼ cup white
    wine vinegar
4 shallots, finely chopped
1 tablespoon chopped fresh tarragon
    leaves
1 tablespoon chopped mixed fresh herbs
    such as parsley, chervil, and chives
Salt and freshly ground black pepper,
    to taste
4 large egg yolks, at room temperature
1 cup (2 sticks) unsalted butter,
    cut into 16 pieces

1. In a small nonreactive saucepan, combine the vinegar, shallots, tarragon and other herbs, and a little salt and pepper. Boil over high heat until the liquid has reduced to about 3 tablespoons, about 10 minutes.

2. Strain the liquid through a fine-mesh sieve into a wide nonreactive bowl that will fit snugly over a saucepan or into the nonreactive top of a double boiler. Set aside to cool. Stir the egg yolks into the reduced vinegar and place the pan over a pot of simmering water.

3. Whisking continuously, add the butter bit by bit, making sure each is well incorporated before adding another piece. Scrape the sides of the bowl as you whisk, and be sure that the eggs don't scramble. (If they should, you can try to save the sauce by picking up the bowl and quickly whisking in a spoonful of hot water—you can take it from the simmering water.) Continue whisking until all the butter is mixed in and the sauce is velvety smooth.

4. Remove the pan from the heat, but leave the bowl or double boiler top over the water so the sauce will stay warm. Whisk it occasionally as it stands to prevent it from breaking or forming a skin.

SAUCE CHORON

MAKES ABOUT 1½ CUPS

Traditionally sauce Choron is made by whisking a small amount of tomato purée into hollandaise sauce. Chef Jamie Shannon makes his by reducing a tomato sauce, then mixing it with béarnaise sauce.

Béarnaise (page 167)
2 tablespoons tomato paste, or
    ¼ cup Tomato Sauce (page 170)
    reduced by half

In a small mixing bowl, stir the ingredients together until well combined. Serve this sauce with fish.

SOUBISE

MAKES ABOUT 2 CUPS

Soubise is an onion purée thickened with béchamel. It is served with roast meats, with croquettes, and with egg dishes.

Béchamel Sauce (facing page)
1 tablespoon unsalted butter
About 1½ cups chopped onions
Salt and freshly ground black pepper,
    to taste
¼ cup heavy (or whipping) cream
    (optional)

1. Start the béchamel sauce, and while it is cooking, melt the butter in a heavy sauté pan that has a lid. Add the onions, stir well, and cook over low heat, covered, until they are totally soft but not browned, 20 minutes.

2. Place the onions in a blender or food processor and purée. When the béchamel sauce is ready, add it and blend well. Season with salt and pepper, and thin the sauce with a little cream, if desired. Serve warm, reheating the sauce if necessary.

BÉCHAMEL SAUCE

MAKES ABOUT 1¼ CUPS

For three hundred years, this basic French white sauce has thickened, bound, and added character to dishes as different as lasagna and croquettes. Though shunned in the trendy 1980s, it has returned to most serious cook's kitchens as a staple. Béchamel is the foundation of many of the sauces of both France and Italy.

2 tablespoons unsalted butter
2 tablespoons all-purpose flour
1½ cups milk
½ teaspoon salt
Freshly ground black pepper
Freshly grated nutmeg (optional)

1. In a heavy saucepan, melt the butter over medium-low heat. Whisk in the flour and cook until it is foamy, about 3 minutes.

2. Pour in the milk all at once, whisking constantly. Raise the heat to medium-high and bring to a boil, whisking constantly. Remove the pan from the heat and add the salt, still whisking. Return the pan to the stove, but over reduced heat. Simmer, whisking occasionally so the mixture doesn't stick or burn, until the sauce is smooth and thick.

3. Remove the sauce from the heat and grind in a little pepper and a hint of nutmeg, if desired. Use as directed.

REDUCED CREAM SAUCES

Boiling cream to thicken it creates the richest sauce you can make, and it's infinitely variable. When serving Scots Eggs hot, I'll often make a quick onion sauce instead of a soubise: I'll put a chopped onion in a cup of cream and simmer it while I prepare the eggs. By the time the dish is finished, I simply strain the sauce through a fine-mesh sieve and season it with a little salt and pepper. You can add fresh or cooked tomatoes, sun-dried tomatoes, peppercorns, fresh herbs, or pan juices to the cream as it thickens. You can also combine the cream with a stock and reduce until thick, but you'll need to add an acid such as lemon juice or sherry vinegar to help bind it. Like béchamel, reduced cream is a lily begging to be gilded.

TOMATO SAUCE

MAKES ABOUT 5 CUPS

This tomato purée is a quick and delicious kitchen basic. The sauce can be flavored with the herbs of your choice; ricotta cheese or cream can be stirred into it too. It nicely complements the fried fish and crab cakes in Chapter 4, or it can be highly spiced, cooled, and used as a cocktail sauce or ketchup.

2 to 3 tablespoons olive oil
1 medium onion, chopped
   (about ¾ cup)
2 cloves garlic, minced
6 vine-ripened tomatoes (about 2
   pounds), peeled, seeded, and
   chopped, or 1 large can (28 ounces)
   plus 1 small can (16 ounces) peeled
   tomatoes, seeded and chopped
1 teaspoon salt
Freshly ground black pepper, to taste
1 bay leaf
Chopped fresh or dried herbs of your
   choice (parsley, sage, thyme, savory,
   oregano), to taste
Freshly squeezed lemon juice, to taste

1. Coat the bottom of a nonreactive saucepan with olive oil, and place over medium heat. When the oil is hot, add the onion and cook until it begins to become transparent, about 5 minutes.

2. Add the garlic, tomatoes, salt, pepper, bay leaf, and herbs. Cook until the sauce has begun to thicken, 15 minutes.

3. Season with the lemon juice. Remove the bay leaf, transfer the sauce to a blender or food processor, and purée. Strain the sauce, if desired, and return it to the pan off the heat. The sauce can be reduced to a thicker consistency. Place it over low heat and watch carefully until it reaches the preferred thickness.

TOMATO SAUCES

Tomato-based sauces are the perfect accompaniments to a variety of the fried foods here. Try both my recipes for tomato sauce—one traditional and one packing some heat (page 172)—with the Fried Mozzarella, Mozzarella Sandwiches, Stuffed Squash Blossoms Tempura, and as a nice change from tartar sauce for crab cakes. Cocktail Sauce can be served with fried seafood and fish. Homemade Salsa is perfect with Tortilla Chips and can also top seafood and vegetables.

SALSA

MAKES ABOUT 1½ CUPS

Salsa simply means "sauce" in Spanish, but this traditional dipping sauce of raw tomato and onion is what most of us think of when we hear the word. This is also referred to as creole sauce—the classic *salsa criolla cruda* of Latin America. Serve with Tortilla Chips (see Index) or fried fish.

1 onion, chopped (about ¾ cup)

1 large ripe tomato, peeled, seeded, and chopped (about ⅔ cup)

1 jalapeño pepper, deribbed, seeded, and chopped

2 cloves garlic, finely minced

Salt and freshly ground black pepper, to taste

Juice of 1 lime

½ to ¾ cup extra-virgin olive oil, to taste

Chopped fresh cilantro leaves, to taste

Combine all the ingredients in a medium-size bowl and allow to sit at room temperature for about 1 hour before serving.

COCKTAIL SAUCE

MAKES ABOUT 1 CUP

Cocktail sauce is one of the easiest sauces to make because you can rely on prepared ketchup for the base. The standard varieties are usually too sweet for my palate, but commercial ketchups now come in a world of flavors. Try to find a hot one or one with little or no sugar. Natural-foods stores carry several brands.

1 cup tomato ketchup

2 tablespoons freshly grated or
   prepared horseradish

2 teaspoons fresh lemon juice

Tabasco or other bottled hot sauce,
   to taste

About 1 hour before you plan to serve the sauce, combine all the ingredients in a small bowl. Refrigerate for about 45 minutes so the flavors can blend. Remove the sauce from the refrigerator about 15 minutes before serving and let it return to room temperature.

GRILLED TOMATO HOT SAUCE

MAKES ABOUT 2 CUPS

This unusual hot sauce is mellowed by the grilling. Use it with French Fries, Fried Mozzarella, Mozzarella Sandwiches, or Stuffed Squash Blossom Tempura (see Index). It's also great with fried fish.

3 large firm-ripe tomatoes (about
   1½ pounds)

2 sweet onions, such as Vidalias
   (about 1 pound), unpeeled

3 large cloves garlic, unpeeled

6 large fresh red or green chile peppers

Salt, to taste

1. Prepare a charcoal fire in a grill, preheat a gas grill to hot, or turn on an oven broiler. If you are using the oven, remove all but one rack and place it on the bottom shelf.

2. Do not peel the vegetables. When the grill is hot, place the vegetables directly over the heat, about 4 inches from the flames. (If you are using an oven, place the vegetables on a baking sheet and place it on the rack.) Grill or broil the vegetables until the skins char and pop, turning them so that they are evenly cooked. Burn only the skins, not the flesh. Remove the vegetables to a cutting surface as they finish grilling, and allow them to cool enough to handle.

3. As the vegetables cool, peel them (no need to seed the tomatoes or chiles). Chop the onions and combine them with the remaining vegetables in a blender or food processor. Purée the sauce to the desired consistency. Add the salt. Serve immediately, or refrigerate, tightly capped, for up to 2 days.

ROASTED PEPPER PUREE

MAKES ABOUT 1¾ CUPS

This delicious sauce goes well with bean or crab cakes. In a rush, you can use prepared roasted peppers. I frequently see jars of them at my grocer's (a 12-ounce jar should do for this recipe); they're often in the deli or take-out case as well.

3 or 4 ripe red bell peppers
2 scallions (including some of the
    green tops), chopped
¾ cup dry white wine
6 sprigs flat-leaf parsley,
    finely chopped
Salt and freshly ground black pepper,
    to taste

1. Roast the peppers: Using a long-handled fork, hold the peppers over a gas flame until the skin blisters and turns black all over.

2. Place the peppers in a plastic bag and close it tight; leave them for about 10 minutes to loosen the charred skins.

3. Meanwhile, combine the scallions and the wine in a nonreactive heavy saucepan, bring to a boil, and reduce by half, 3 to 5 minutes.

4. Place the peppers on a cutting board and peel away their skins. Seed them by pulling the stem end away from the pod; most of the seeds will pull out. Scrape any remaining seeds off with the blade of a knife; do *not* put the peppers under running water.

PEPPER SAUCE

Like tomatoes, capsicum peppers were discovered in the New World and forever changed the cooking of Europe. The sweet bells, pimientos, and cubanelles are actually very closely related to the fiery hot chilies—if you grow peppers at home you must be aware of the cross pollination. (I've had bland cayennes that grew next to bells, and vice-versa). These wonderful condiments are all simple to make and range from the velvety sweet red pepper purée to the fiery hot sauces of the Caribbean and Mexico. Be sure to check out the hot Asian sauces as well.

5. Combine the parsley, the peppers, and the wine reduction in a blender and purée until smooth. Season to taste with salt and pepper, and use immediately.

CARIBBEAN LIME SAUCE

MAKES ABOUT 1 CUP

There are as many hot sauces in the Caribbean as there are islands, but this simple chile sauce for seafood is a favorite. It's not a good keeper, so serve it fresh.

1 medium onion, chopped
   (about 1 cup)
About ½ cup fresh lime juice
2 tablespoons unsalted butter
2 cloves garlic, minced
2 jalapeño peppers, deribbed, seeded,
   and finely chopped
Salt, to taste

1. Place the onion in a nonreactive container and cover with the lime juice; set aside for 1 hour. Then drain the onion, reserving the juice.

2. Melt the butter in a small skillet over medium-low heat. Add the onion and cook slowly until translucent, about 15 minutes.

3. Add the garlic and jalapeños, raise the heat to high, and cook for 1 minute. Pour the mixture into the reserved lime juice. Stir well to blend, then add salt to taste. Serve immediately.

IN THE PANTRY

America's fascination with hot sauces is at an all-time high. There are literally hundreds of bottled sauces on the market, and many of them are excellent. Fried foods beg for spiciness, so find one or two prepared sauces that you like and keep them on hand.

BASIC HOT PEPPER SAUCE

MAKES ABOUT 1 CUP

Here's the basic formula for a hot pepper sauce. You can add puréed fruit, such as mango or papaya, as they do in Jamaica. You can add spices such as caraway, and pound the mixture with a mortar and pestle to form a paste, as they do in Tunisia. Hot sauces *should* vary: every cook has his or her own level of heat tolerance, and chiles, even those from the same plant, vary in potency.

Obviously the choice of pepper will greatly affect this recipe. Anaheim or New Mexico are mildly bittersweet; jalapeños taste like bell peppers but can have a very hot bite; poblanos have an herbal flavor (anchos are the dried form).

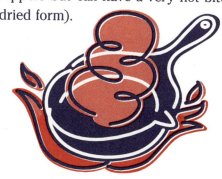

**10 to 12 fresh or dried hot red or
    green chile peppers**
¼ cup olive oil
1 large onion, chopped (about 1 cup)
4 cloves garlic, minced
½ teaspoon whole cumin seeds
½ teaspoon whole coriander seeds
Salt, to taste

1. If you are using fresh chiles, roast them (see page 173 steps 1 and 2). Using rubber gloves, stem, skin, and seed the peppers. If you are using dried peppers, remove the seeds and stems, cut the peppers into strips, and add boiling water just to cover; set aside for 20 minutes.

2. Meanwhile, pour the oil into a sauté pan and place it over medium heat. Add the onion and cook until softened, 5 to 10 minutes.

3. Place the garlic, cumin, and coriander in a blender and grind with quick bursts until the spices are evenly ground. Add the peppers and their soaking water (if any) and purée. Add the purée to the onion.

4. Simmer the sauce for about 1 hour, or until it has reduced by half. Allow to cool to room temperature, then season with the salt. You can blend the sauce again for a smoother consistency, if desired. Serve immediately or store, tightly capped, in the refrigerator for up to 2 weeks.

TOMATILLO SAUCE

MAKES ABOUT 2½ CUPS

This is the classic green sauce—*salsa verde*—of Mexico. It's delicious with chips or seafood. If you can't find fresh tomatillos, look for canned ones in the Mexican foods section of your supermarket.

Serve it right away, since this is best when freshly made.

1 pound (12 to 16) fresh tomatillos, husked and rinsed, or 1 can (13 ounces) tomatillos, drained
1 small onion, chopped (about ¼ cup)
2 cloves garlic, minced
1 or 2 jalapeño or serrano chiles, stemmed (but not seeded) and chopped
½ to ¾ cup fresh cilantro leaves, or to taste
¼ to ½ cup fresh lime juice or water
Pinch of sugar
Salt, to taste

1. Put the tomatillos, onion, garlic, chiles, and cilantro in a blender with ¼ cup of the lime juice. Purée with quick pulses on high speed until the mixture is smooth; add more liquid if necessary. The sauce can be slightly chunky.

2. Add the sugar and salt, pulse the mixture once again, and serve immediately.

NANCIE'S SWEET-HOT GARLIC SAUCE

MAKES ABOUT 1¼ CUPS

This recipe is adapted from Nancie McDermott's cookbook *Real Thai*. Though the sauce is an authentic one from Thailand, it is awfully close to the hot pepper–vinegar barbecue sauces of Nancie's home state, North Carolina. Serve it with all sorts of fried foods or with spareribs.

The ground fresh chile paste is called by different names in different cultures, but all varieties are basically a combination of ground chiles, vinegar, and salt. Some include garlic as well. Look for half-pint plastic jars of chile paste; the Vietnamese version, *tuong ot,* is widely available (Sriracha is a popular Vietnamese brand). A chunky version with seeds, *tuong ot toi Vietnam,* is made in California. The Indonesian version, *sambal oelek,* is also made in the States. If you can find none of these, make a purée of hot red chiles, garlic, and salt, with just enough vinegar to make it pliable. Or you can use any other hot pepper sauce, such as Tabasco.

1 cup sugar
½ cup water
⅔ cup white vinegar
2 tablespoons minced garlic
1 teaspoon salt
1 tablespoon ground fresh chile paste
    (see headnote), chile-garlic sauce,
    or hot pepper sauce

1. In a small heavy saucepan, combine the sugar, water, vinegar, garlic, and salt. Bring to a rolling boil over medium heat, stirring to dissolve the sugar and salt. Reduce the heat and simmer until the liquid is syrupy but not as thick as honey, about 25 minutes. Remove from the heat and stir in the chile paste. Cool to room temperature.

2. Use immediately or store, tightly sealed, at room temperature for 2 or 3 days or in the refrigerator for up to 2 weeks.

ASIAN DIPPING SAUCES

SPICY VIETNAMESE FISH SAUCE

MAKES ABOUT 1¼ CUPS

This sauce is very similar to the chile-lime sauces of the Caribbean, with the addition of *nuoc mam,* the bottled fish sauce so prevalent in Southeast Asia. Nuoc mam is now available in most supermarkets; the Thai version is called *nam pla.* Tiparos is a widely distributed brand from Bangkok, with average pungency. Because fish sauces vary greatly in potency, you can substitute some water for all or part of the vinegar if the sauce seems too strong for you. Grated carrot and daikon are sometimes added to the sauce. It is used as a dip for all sorts of deep-fried snacks and spring rolls.

2 fresh red chile peppers
4 cloves garlic
3 tablespoons sugar
¼ cup fresh lime juice
½ cup Asian fish sauce,
    such as *nuoc mam* or
    nam pla
½ cup rice vinegar or water
1 large carrot, peeled
    (optional)

1. Wearing rubber gloves, stem, seed, and derib the chiles. Place them in a mortar with the garlic and sugar, and pound until you have a coarse paste.

2. In a small mixing bowl, stir together the chile paste, lime juice, and fish sauce. Add about half of the vinegar and taste the sauce with a piece of the carrot; add the remaining vinegar or water to taste. Then grate the carrot into the sauce, if desired. Use immediately.

TEMPURA DIPPING SAUCE

MAKES ABOUT 2 CUPS

Authentic tempura dipping sauces always contain some *dashi,* a broth made from seaweed and dried bonito tuna flakes, both available in many supermarkets as well as Asian groceries.

1 square (3 inches) dried kelp *(kombu)*
1½ cups cold water
¼ cup dried bonito, flaked
    (katsuobushi)
¼ cup *mirin* (sweet sake), or
    3 tablespoons pale dry sherry
    plus 1 tablespoon sugar
¼ cup Japanese or light soy sauce
1 tablespoon grated fresh ginger

1. Make the *dashi:* Place the kelp and water in a saucepan and bring to a boil over high heat. Immediately stir in the bonito flakes and reduce the heat. Simmer for 5 minutes, then strain into a bowl.

2. Allow the dashi to cool completely unless you are using sherry and sugar in place of the *mirin, i*n which case, stir the sugar into the hot dashi.

3. Add the *mirin* or sherry, soy sauce, and ginger. Stir well, then serve or store in the refrigerator, covered, for up to 1 week.

QUICK TEMPURA DIPPING SAUCE

MAKES ABOUT 2 CUPS

This typical salty and sour dipping sauce can be used with all sorts of fried or steamed dumplings, seafood, and vegetables. This is one of my favorite dipping sauces because it takes practically no time to prepare, and it packs a double punch of hot chilies and ginger.

¼ cup warm *dashi* (see step1, page 179)
    or water
1 tablespoon sugar
1¼ cups soy sauce
¼ cup sake or dry sherry
1 tablespoon grated fresh ginger
1 tablespoon sesame oil
1 teaspoon hot chile oil
About 2 tablespoons fresh lemon
    juice or rice vinegar, to taste

1. In a small mixing bowl, pour the warm *dashi* over the sugar and stir to dissolve. Add the soy sauce, sake, ginger, and both sesame and chile oils. Stir well.

2. Add the lemon juice, and serve or store in the refrigerator, covered, for up to 1 week.

SIDE DISHES

CUCUMBER AND
YOGURT SALAD

SERVES 4

Refreshing *raitas* of cucumber and yogurt appear in India to complement the highly seasoned main dishes. In Greece the dish is served as a cooling appetizer; in Turkey it's puréed and served as a soup. I find that it's a perfect complement to fried foods of all sorts. Serve it in place of potato salad or coleslaw, or as a dressing alongside fritters, such as the Zucchini Pancakes (see Index). Use whatever fresh herb best complements the main dish you are serving. Dill is good alone; parsley, mint, and cilantro go together well.

2 large cucumbers
Salt
1 tablespoon olive oil
2 cloves garlic, chopped
1 cup plain yogurt
3 tablespoons chopped fresh cilantro,
    mint, parsley, or dill (see headnote)

1. Peel the cucumbers and slice them in half lengthwise. Scoop out each half and discard the seeds. Cut the cucumbers into several strips and place them in a colander. Sprinkle them heavily with salt, and allow to drain for 30 minutes.

2. Heat the oil in a small pan over medium heat. Add the garlic and cook for about 3 minutes, but do not let it brown. Place the yogurt in a small bowl and add the oil and garlic. Stir well to combine. Add the herbs and mix in well.

3. Shake off excess water from the cucumbers and place on a cutting surface. Dice them, add to the yogurt, and stir to combine. Cover the bowl and chill well, for at least an hour, before serving.

COLESLAW

SERVES 6

This coleslaw is prepared with a sweetened vinegar solution and is a superior accompaniment to spicy fried seafood or chicken. If you want to add mayonnaise or other seasonings to the slaw, simply drain off the excess liquid and add them to suit your taste. The real beauty of this dish is that it keeps a long time, so you can make it well in advance. Don't be alarmed by the large amount of liquid; just serve it with a slotted spoon. Make the slaw the day before you plan to serve it; it needs time to rest and mellow.

1 cup water
1 cup white vinegar
¾ cup sugar
1½ pounds (about 1 small or ½ large head) green cabbage, grated
1 medium white onion, finely chopped
1 small or ½ large green bell pepper, cored, seeded, and finely chopped
1 small carrot, peeled and grated

2 teaspoons salt
2 teaspoons mustard seeds

1. Combine the water, vinegar, and sugar in a saucepan and bring to a boil, stirring to dissolve the sugar. Set aside to cool.

2. Toss the remaining ingredients well in a large mixing bowl, and pour the cooled vinegar solution over them. Mix well, cover, and refrigerate for at least 24 hours before serving.

CHUNKY FRUIT SALSA

SERVES 4

This is what we call a relish in the South. It's made like the classic raw tomato salsa of Latin America, with bite-size chunks of soft fresh fruit, but it could be made just as easily with cooked black beans or black-eyed peas, with citrus fruits, or with pineapple.

Serve it alongside fritters, such as the Black-Eyed Pea Cakes (see Index), with fried fish, with croquettes or crab cakes, or with chips.

This is typical of the new foods of south Florida, heavily influenced by the Caribbean's love of garlic, lime, and chiles.

**2 mangoes or 4 peaches, peeled,
pitted, and cut into bite-size chunks**
1 cup chopped mild onion
**1 or 2 jalapeño chiles, deribbed,
seeded, and finely chopped,
to taste**
1 clove garlic, minced
½ cup finely chopped red bell pepper
⅓ cup fresh lime juice
**¼ cup fresh mint or cilantro leaves,
or a combination**
Salt, to taste

Toss all the ingredients together in a nonreactive container and allow to sit at room temperature for 30 minutes before serving. Refrigerated, it will keep for up to 3 days.

FRIED RICE

SERVES 4

Most of the Asians I know cook fried rice as a way to quickly assemble a meal from leftovers, not as company food. Many Asian restaurants in this country serve fried rice as a side dish as a matter of course, but I find that it's a simple one-course meal when I'm too tired to *really* cook. You can use pork, chicken, or shrimp with the dish and vary the seasoning to suit your palate. Pork and chicken should be cut into thin, uniform slices, about ½ inch wide.

It's best to make fried rice with cold leftover rice. I prefer to use jasmine rice from Thailand, which is a nutty and fragrant long-grain white rice, or the American-grown Jasmati, but you can use any plain long-grain rice.

You can also use just about any meats and vegetables—raw or leftover cooked; just make sure that all the pieces are cut into shapes that will heat evenly. Add raw vegetables such as snow peas or bell peppers just after the meat; cooked ones should be added after the rice. Use this recipe as a guideline.

1 tablespoon Asian fish sauce,
    such as *nam pla* (see Note)
1 tablespoon soy sauce
½ teaspoon sugar
1 or 2 chile peppers, such as jalapeño,
    deribbed, seeded, and chopped,
    to taste
4 cups cooked long-grain white rice,
    preferably chilled
3 tablespoons vegetable oil
2 cloves garlic, chopped
¾ cup chopped onion or scallions
½ pound thinly sliced pork or
    chicken or peeled medium shrimp,
    cooked or uncooked
1 cup small broccoli florets, slivered
    bell pepper, or snow peas, cooked
    or uncooked
1 large egg, beaten

1. Mix the fish sauce, soy sauce, sugar, and chiles in a small cup and set aside. Rub the rice between your fingers, breaking up any lumps into individual grains; set aside.

2. Heat a wok over high heat and add the oil, swirling it around to coat the surface. When the oil is very hot, add the garlic and toss until it is golden, just a few seconds. Add the onions and toss until they begin to soften, about 1 minute. Then, add the uncooked meat or shrimp, along with any uncooked vegetables, and stir-fry for about 2 minutes. The meat should no longer be pink.

3. Add the egg and tilt the wok so that the egg spreads out into a thin layer. As soon as it begins to set, scramble it to break it up. Then quickly add the rice, tossing it around to thoroughly coat the grains. At this point add any cooked vegetables or meats to the dish, stirring well to evenly distribute all the ingredients. Add a little of the prepared sauce to the wok and toss well. As soon as all the ingredients are warmed through, the fried rice is ready to serve. Pass the remaining sauce as a seasoning.

Note: Asian fish sauces—*nam pla* and *nuoc mam*—are available in Asian markets and the Asian sections of many supermarkets.

STEAMED RICE

SERVES 6

Plain steamed rice invites a world of accompaniments. It is *the* sidekick for pan-fried chicken in much of the South, where it's covered with the gravy made from the pan drippings. Many of the famous sautéed and stir-fried dishes of the world would be incomplete without rice, yet it's amazing how many good cooks and restaurant chefs serve tasteless instant or converted rice.

Nothing could be simpler to prepare than a pot of perfectly steamed rice, cooked so that each grain stands separately. The secret is to never stir the rice with a spoon. A pot of rice can be flavored any number of ways—by cooking it in stock instead of water or by adding chopped herbs, tomatoes, sautéed aromatic vegetables, nuts, or lemon zest once the cooking is completed.

4 cups water
½ teaspoon salt
2 cups long-grain white rice

1. At least 30 minutes before you plan to serve the rice, bring the water to a boil in a 2-quart pot that has a tight-fitting lid. Add the salt and the rice. Stir once with a fork to distribute the rice evenly, but do not stir it again.

2. Adjust the heat so that the rice simmers (bubbles just barely break the surface) but no more than simmers. Cook the rice, covered, for exactly 13 minutes, never lifting the lid.

3. Turn off the heat and let the rice stand, still covered, for another 12 minutes to steam. Leave the pot alone until you're ready to serve the rice.

4. To serve, lift the lid and fluff the rice with a large fork (never a spoon) to further separate the grains, which should be all but dry.

BASIC GRITS

SERVES 2 TO 4

Many southerners use grits the way Italians use pasta and the Chinese use rice—as a foundation upon which sauces of all sorts appear. Fried fish are often served with a big plateful of grits. Shrimp and grits is traditional breakfast or supper fare in Savannah and Charleston. And in Louisiana, *grillades*—tough cuts of meat pounded, braised with tomatoes, and served with grits—are favored Creole fare.

The fried grits cakes in Chapter 2 are popular too, but you'll have to learn to cook *real* grits first. Please try to find whole-grain grits, stone-ground from organically grown corn, to use in this recipe; supermarket grits are not, in my opinion, edible.

When the grits are almost done, you can turn the heat down to its lowest setting and cover the pan while you prepare the rest of the meal. Or you can continue with the recipe for Basic Grits Cakes (see Index), which are enriched, breaded, and fried to a golden brown and topped with all sorts of delicious sauces.

This basic recipe uses water as the cooking medium, but you can substitute milk, cream, half-and-half, or stock for some or all of the liquid. In fact, if you plan to serve the grits plain, a little stock made from trimmings from the main course is a welcome addition; stir it in near the end of the cooking time.

---

4 cups water
2 tablespoons unsalted butter
Salt, to taste
1 cup stone-ground whole-grain grits
   (see Sources, page 189)

1. Bring the water, butter, and salt to a boil in a saucepan.

2. Gradually add the grits and return to a boil. Reduce the heat to a simmer and cook the grits, uncovered, stirring occasionally so that they do not stick or form a skin, until they are creamy and done to your liking. It takes about 25 minutes, but many people like to cook them much longer (the longer they cook, the creamier they get). If you do, you may have to add more liquid.

3. Serve the grits piping hot, with butter, gravy, or your favorite sauce, such as a cream reduction (page 169).

NEW POTATO SALAD

SERVES 6 TO 8

I f you're taking fried chicken on a picnic, or simply having a dinner of fried fish, make up a batch of this old standby to serve alongside. Down South, we usually use a sweet pickle in the salad to balance the hot seasonings of the main dish. If the dish it's accompanying is mildly seasoned, use dill pickle instead.

2 pounds new potatoes, scrubbed
    and halved or cut into 1½-inch
    wedges, boiled, and cooled
3 hard-cooked eggs, chopped
1½ cups finely chopped celery
1 medium onion, finely chopped
½ cup Blender Mayonnaise
    (page 162)
1 heaping tablespoon prepared
    mustard
½ cup finely chopped pickles,
    sweet or dill (see headnote)
Salt and freshly ground black pepper,
    to taste
Cayenne pepper, to taste
1 to 2 tablespoons chopped fresh herbs
    of your choice (basil, dill, savory,
    parsley), to taste
½ teaspoon paprika

1. In a large mixing bowl, combine the potatoes, eggs, celery, onion, mayonnaise, mustard, and pickles. Season with salt, black pepper, and cayenne. Cover and refrigerate, for up to 3 days, until ready to serve.

2. Just before serving, add the herbs to the salad and mix well. Dust the top with paprika, and serve.

MASHED POTATOES

SERVES 4

Home cooks throughout the country make gravy with the drippings from pan-frying. In the coastal South, where once there were rice plantations, that gravy is still served over rice. In most of the country, however, mashed potatoes are the norm.

Mashed potatoes can be made with the water in which the potatoes were boiled or with milk, but I am partial to this creamy version.

4 baking potatoes (about ¾ pound each),
    peeled and cut into ½-inch wedges
2 teaspoons salt
1 cup heavy (or whipping) cream
Gravy, for serving

1. In a large saucepan, cover the potatoes with water. Add the salt and bring to a boil. Boil until the potatoes are soft but not translucent, about 10 minutes.

2. Meanwhile, bring the cream to a boil in a small pot; then take it off the heat.

3. When the potatoes are done, immediately drain them of all water. Thoroughly mash them with a potato masher, an electric mixer, or a heavy wire whisk, adding the hot cream a little at a time. Serve with lots of gravy.

SOURCES

CORN PRODUCTS

Stone-ground grits, corn meal, and corn flour are all available from **Hoppin' John's®**, my culinary bookstore. I also now sell a variety of South Carolina specialty foods such as bottled hot sauces, my own line of condiments, benne wafers, etc. Write or call:

30 Pinckney Street

Charleston SC 29401

(803) 577-6404 or Fax: (803) 577-6932.

MASA HARINA

Masa Harina is ground pesole, the Southwest's version of hominy or corn that is treated with slaked lime. It is widely available in supermarkets.

FLOUR AND CRACKER MEAL

Soft southern flour is made from low-gluten winter wheat. It is available from **White Lily Foods.** Call or write to find a distributor in your area:

PO Box 871

Knoxville TN 37901

(800) 264-5459

or visit their web site at

http://www.whitelily.com.

It is also available from Williams-Sonoma.

SEMOLINA FLOUR

Semolina flour is made from hard durum wheat. It makes excellent homemade pasta. **NOW Foods** distributes an excellent product that is widely available in natural-foods stores and many supermarkets. For a distributor in your area, call or write:

550 West Mitchell Drive

Glendale Heights, IL 60139-2581

(800) 283-3500.

CRACKER MEAL

Martha White Foods makes an unadulterated cracker meal that is a superior coating for fried pork chops and shrimp. Call to find a distributor in your area:

(800) 663-6317.

CONVERSION TABLE

U.S. DRY & LIQUID MEASURES

The following equivalents are based on U.S. fluid measure, since in the U.S. measurements for dry ingredients, as well as for liquid, are by volume, not by weight.

1 pinch = less than ⅛ teaspoon (dry)

1 dash = 3 drops to scant ⅛ teaspoon (liquid)

3 teaspoons = 1 tablespoon (dry and liquid)

2 tablespoons = 1 ounce (liquid)

4 tablespoons = ¼ cup = 1 ounce (liquid)

5⅓ tablespoons = ⅓ cup (dry and liquid)

8 tablespoons = ½ cup = 4 ounces (liquid)

16 tablespoons = 1 cup = 8 ounces (liquid)

2 cups = 16 ounces (liquid) = 1 pint (liquid)

4 cups = 32 ounces (liquid) = 1 quart (liquid)

16 cups = 128 ounces (liquid) = 1 gallon (liquid)

TEMPERATURES

°Fahrenheit (F) to °Celsius (C)

− 10°F = − 23.3°C (freezer storage)

  0°F = − 17.7°C

 32°F =   0°C (water freezes)

 50°F =   10°C

 68°F =   20°C (room temperature)

100°F =   37.7°C

150°F =   65.5°C

205°F =   96.1°C (water simmers)

212°F = 100°C (water boils)

300°F = 148.8°C

325°F = 162.8°C

350°F = 177°C (baking)

375°F = 190.5°C

400°F = 204.4°C (hot oven)

425°F = 218.3°C

450°F = 232°C (very hot oven)

475°F = 246.1°C

500°F = 260°C (broiling)

APPROXIMATE EQUIVALENTS

1 quart (liquid) = about 1 liter

1 stick butter = 8 tablespoons = 4 ounces = ½ cup

1 cup all-purpose presifted flour = 5 ounces

1 cup stone-ground yellow cornmeal = 4½ ounces

1 cup granulated sugar = 7 ounces

1 cup (packed) brown sugar = 6 ounces

1 cup confectioners' sugar = 4½ ounces

1 large egg = 2 ounces = about ¼ cup

1 egg yolk = about 1 tablespoon

1 egg white = about 2 tablespoons

CONVERSION FACTORS

If you need to convert measurements into their equivalents in another system, here's how to do it.

ounces to grams: multiply ounce figure by 28.35 to get number of grams

grams to ounces: multiply gram figure by .0353 to get number of ounces

pounds to grams: multiply pound figure by 453.59 to get number of grams

pounds to kilograms: multiply pound figure by 0.45 to get number of kilograms

ounces to milliliters: multiply ounce figure by 29.57 to get number of milliliters

cups to liters: multiply cup figure by 0.24 to get number of liters

Fahrenheit to Celsius: subtract 32 from the Fahrenheit figure, multiply by 5, then divide by 9 to get Celsius figure

Celsius to Fahrenheit: multiply Celsius figure by 9, divide by 5, then add 32 to get Fahrenheit figure

inches to centimeters: multiply inch figure by 2.54 to get number of centimeters

centimeters to inches: multiply centimeter figure by 0.39 to get number of inches

INDEX